'Tears In The Sand'

Dear Liz,

I hope you enjoy the book.

[signature]

Steven Rigby

authorHOUSE®

AuthorHouse™ UK Ltd.
500 Avebury Boulevard
Central Milton Keynes, MK9 2BE
www.authorhouse.co.uk
Phone: 08001974150

First published by AuthorHouse 2/14/2011

ISBN: 978-1-4567-7349-6 (sc)
ISBN: 978-1-4567-7350-2 (e)

Acknowledgments

This little book, the account of my journey of a lifetime, was only made possible, thanks to several people it would be remiss of me not to thank.

Kevin and Audrey James, whose love, time and effort were greatly rewarded, by me growing into a different and more enlightened person. Their friendship I shall always treasure.

Vee, whose encouragement from beginning to end and whose help and assistance made all things easy.

Sandy Mactaggart, whose generosity goes beyond the norm, in allowing a complete stranger such as I, to make use of his holiday home.

Ilona, my wife, for giving me the freedom and space to explore something new and as a result, to 'Soar On Eagles Wings'.

Bob, who reminded me that it's never too late to do new things and to try that which might be considered impossible.

Day 1.

Thursday August the 6th 2009 and my journey of a lifetime, my adventure of a lifetime is soon to begin. My bag, which has been packed for several day's, is sitting on the settee, along with all the other bits I expect I might need for the holiday. I have checked that my passport, money and other logistical information required, contact telephone numbers, in case of any unforeseen emergency and so on, are safe and in an easy to reach place for when they are required.

My father was a worrier as am I. My stomach feels as though it's turning in slow circles and even though I've received confirmation that the taxi is coming for 11am, the agreed time and that I have everything I need, there is that constant nagging feeling at the back of my mind that something has yet to be done, that I have missed something or that something dramatic is about to go wrong!

It's only 10am, but I have decided that hanging around my home, watching the clock slowly tick bye, is not the healthiest thing for me right now, so I head for my van and drive off to the next village down the road, Draycott, to collect Vee who has agreed to be my PA for the holiday. Finding Vee was a major part in my being able to go on this holiday and I have a dear friend of my wife and I to thank for introducing her to me.

It had been a dream of mine to have one of those holidays of a lifetime that you're always hearing about and whilst serving in the army, I had planned after completing my time, to take such a break to the Caribbean, a location that had always appealed to me. Unfortunately, I broke my neck during an army gymnastic display on the 11th of July 1981 and that for me, or so I thought at that time, meant the end of all my dreams. I, like many I assumed, had my life planned out for the next forty odd years. They ran from, the moment I signed on as a new recruit in the Royal Artillery in late 1977, done with the sole intention of becoming a PT Instructor, right through to my leaving after serving my time, to settling down. Those dreams though, were changed in a blink of an eye and my plans dramatically altered. So, for the next twenty odd years, in coming to terms with my injury and settling, for what I presumed to be the best that life could offer me given the circumstances, holidays were restricted to making use of the respite facilities offered to disabled ex-service men, in a hospital home in Worthing West Sussex. I had tried travel abroad fairly early into my disability, but felt left out as a wheelchair user. But then a friend, knowing of my desire to travel further abroad than Worthing, encouraged me to try for that dream holiday. After all, the range of possibilities for travel had altered in a big way since my early attempts and it was time for me to catch up. So that was what I decided to do.

In the year 2004, the year of my 50th birthday, I started making tentative plans with regard to taking the plunge in sorting out my break. The first thing for me to consider was a P.A. (Personal Assistant) My level of disability, means that I am unable to totally care for myself, I regard myself as about 90% independent and only then in my home environment. Going abroad would mean that that figure would change for the worse and so I was definitely going to need some assistance. As it happened, I had kept in touch with someone, a Kerry Ann Smedburg, who had previously worked for a care agency who looked after me and so she knew my care needs very well. After putting the idea to her, about her coming along as my P.A., she first of all considered the idea and then agreed. With for me, the biggest obstacle to going away sorted, I then went to my local travel shop and discussed my needs and where I wanted to go. After just over an hour, I was booked into an all-inclusive, wheelchair accessible resort, with upper class flights to Trinidad and Tabago. With my deposit paid, there was nothing else to do but wait for the off date. A few months later a bombshell blew up under my plans. Kerry Ann, a happily married woman, rang me to say she was pregnant and that she could no longer come with me! Whilst I was at the same time really pleased for her and her good news, I was devastated by the fact that I only had a few weeks to try and find a replacement. Now you would imagine finding someone to help care for someone on a holiday of this nature to be a breeze, but try as I might, I could not find anyone interested in coming along. So my dream vanished along with the deposit I had paid.

Four years later, one evening in a pub where my mate Bob and I meet regularly for a beer and a chat, the conversation eventually got around to the awful summer we had all just endured and our hopes for things being better in terms of the weather in future years. We have both had disappointing breaks due to the bad weather in the previous years and we were expressing our wishes for something more memorable. Bob then brought up my desire for the exotic holiday I had always wanted and when I began to dismiss it, saying that it was too late and I was now too old to really enjoy it, he got annoyed with me and kept on at me. He kept encouraging me to have another crack at it, saying I would regret never having achieved it. By the end of the evening, in order to shut him up, I had agreed to go again to my local travel shop, to start over the process of booking myself my dream holiday. Two days after that meeting, I sat in my study and as usual turned my computer on to check my emails. There was one from a guy who had done some work for ITV, the television station; he had been to our home doing an interview, which had been broadcast several months ago in regard to my marriage and our on-going love story. My wife and I had got married in March 1984, after a huge international press story. This was brought about because the Catholic Church initially refused us permission to marry, stating that because I was disabled, I was, in their view, unable to properly consummate the marriage and therefore unable to have children. This was something the Church, it seemed to me and obviously the press at that time, regarded as the only purpose for marriage and over the years following 1984, we have regularly appeared in the press or on TV with follow up stories. Anyway, his email had a request from someone claiming to know me from my army days, a Kevin James who, after seeing the TV programme, wanted to make contact again with me and was it all right to pass on my telephone number to him. Curious, because in truth I could not put a face to the name, I gave him my permission to pass on my number and thought nothing more about it.

Two days later, on the eve of my going to the travel shop, my phone rang and I found myself in conversation with Kevin. He introduced himself and asked if I remembered him and truthfully I told him no, to which he replied that it was to be expected and understandable as it was over 27 years since we had last met. He went on to say that we had been at Aldershot together at the time of my accident and that in fact he had been right behind me and had seen exactly what happened to me. Now I had, ever since the accident, brought forward many theories as to how I had broken my neck, but had never been able to conclusively answer any of my own questions as to how it had happened. Kevin was now telling me he knew all the answers, because he saw it take place. The conversation moved on to how busy I was and what sort of things did I do to occupy my time, to how and where did I take my breaks. I then filled him in as to my respite breaks in Worthing and he quite casually asked if I fancied joining him for a couple of weeks. I then asked what he did for a living and where he was? I knew it was somewhere overseas, because there had been a delay in our conversation, one you get when talking to someone a great distance away. He then replied, that he managed a private island for a very rich individual in the Bahamas! and that the owner was happy for them, Kevin and his wife Audrey, to have guests of their own staying on the island. At this point in the conversation my mind was a whirl, was this a windup, was a friend having a laugh, could this really be happening to me so soon after my making the decision to try again for my dream holiday?

Well it was true and our phone conversation ended with reassurances from him, that all would be done to make my time with them on the island, a wonderful one. So once again, my search was on to try and find a P.A. who would be willing to spend two weeks on a private island in the Bahamas, looking after me for the two hours a day of actual care that I needed!

In going about my search, I let it be known amongst all my friends and acquaintances that I was hoping to go away the following year, the summer of 2009. Of course they all said they would love to come but I knew they were not really serious and I began to have my doubts about finding someone, until, the good friend I talked of earlier, a Mrs Val Barton, who was at that time one of my main carers, happened to mention that she had been talking about me and my holiday to someone she knew who was a nurse in her local pub. Her name was Veronica, but preferred to be known as Vee and she seemed agreeable to the idea. So then began the process of exchanging telephone numbers and making plans to meet to discuss what was hopefully about to happen in the following months, making this dream holiday of mine a reality.

Having now arrived outside Vee's home in my van, I phone her and within a few minutes she has loaded her bags and we are heading back to my place to await the taxi. It's only 10.45 am, but it appears as I drive around the corner into my street, that the taxi has already arrived, which to me is great. I hate waiting and had he arrived later than 11.00 am as arranged, I would have really started to feel sick in my stomach. As it happens, by the time I have parked my van and we have introduced ourselves, retrieved my bags from the house, got helped into the car followed by my manual wheelchair and all our bags, had the power chair I normally use all day taken back into the house and locked up and actually started our journey to Heathrow airport, it is bang on 11.00 am.

The journey down the M1 was fairly uneventful. It's a bright, if slightly cloudy day and I'm sitting comfortably with my head to my left allowing the sun, when it does come from behind the clouds, to warm my face. It's a strange sensation for me to be a passenger. As a disabled person who uses a power chair pretty much every day, there are very few occasions, where in order to get from A-B, I don't drive myself, so, sitting in Charlie's Vauxhall Astra Estate, I find it hard to relax. I'm tired because I'm so excited and so worked up about this trip, that trying to get to sleep last night had been difficult and I can clearly remember waking up several times during the night worrying about one aspect or another of the two weeks ahead. But even though I am tired, the driver part of me keeps me awake, with one eye on the road ahead. Charlie though is a good driver and a good foil to my worries as he chats about his work, his life and this helps me to relax enough to close my eyes occasionally. Before too long, it's around 1.30 pm and we are pulling into a space next to the dropping off zone of the new terminal 5 at Heathrow airport.

Between Vee and Charlie, they quickly get me into my red lightweight manual chair. Then, having loaded our bags into a trolley and paid Charlie the agreed fare for this leg of the two-way trip and having repeated our return date and approximate time of arrival, so we all know where and when we shall be meeting up for our homeward journey, Vee and I set off for the check in desk. Airports are big places and getting about usually involves a good walk to get to where you have to and even though I was on four wheels, I found it tough going. My chair is not the best and has always drifted to the left when freewheeling; this meant it required constant corrections to keep it going in a straight line. Also, having not been in it for any length of time in quite a while, I'm not used to the energy it requires to push it, so, after only a few minutes, I'm exhausted and hang onto the trolley, leaving Vee to push it and pull me.

We queue at the computerised ticket check in and are helped by a member of staff, who then directs us to a baggage check in desk about a mile away? Poor Vee must be wondering how the rest of the holiday is going to be, based on how useless I am at the moment, but I also think that she knows I'm tired and nervous based on previous chats and appears happy to do the lugging about. With my chair now proudly displaying the correct baggage ticket, ready for it's installation into the hold of the plane, once I'm out of it, we are again directed to an area, where anyone requiring special assistance, waits to be helped according to their particular needs. Within a few minutes, another member of staff is pushing my chair to the security check queue, giving Vee a rest and once through there, she pushes me to the reserved lounge. We are travelling 'Club World' and this lounge is one of the perks, offering you a relaxed place to wait for final boarding, with plenty of choice of food and drink to help yourself too and to help while away the time. I thought it quite strange to offer free drink, as the news is full of problems with passengers being denied access to flights because of too much alcohol consumption. Still feeling anxious about the next few hours, I restricted myself to a couple of rolls, which I didn't enjoy because they were hard and crusty and a glass of juice. One glass only, because one of the major worries I had was going to the toilet on the plane, something that would not be possible for me. I was therefore restricting my fluid intake, so that my bladder would not overfill. This is not an ideal thing for my disability and me, but one that I felt was necessary in the short term. I told myself that I could quickly catch up with fluid intake once we have arrived. Our flight was due to take off at 5.15 pm, so we have a few hours to kill and drinking is not on the agenda for me.

Vee has a book with her and I turn to the window nearby and do what thousands of other travellers have done before me, which is to watch the planes land and take off and the bustle of life in a major airport below me.

We were told by the woman who pushed me to the lounge, that nearer the time for boarding, someone would search us out to escort us to the departure lounge and as our flight time drew nearer and nearer, once again the knots began to twist in my stomach and my thoughts drifted to all manner of things that might go wrong. They might miss us in the crowd; no one had passed the message on about my needing an escort, all of which ended with the same scenario, which was that the plane would go without us. To alleviate some of my concerns, I suggested to Vee, that, after a visit to the toilet to drain of what little there was in my leg bag, we should move nearer to the reception desk of the reserved lounge. Having done that, I made sure that I had a good view of the reception desk and them of me. Ten or fifteen minutes or so later, around 4.00 pm, someone was making a beeline towards us, a young guy who asked if my name was Mr Rigby and after receiving confirmation, explained that he was there to push me down to the departure lounge, in readiness to board the plane.

It was pouring with rain as I looked out of the windows of the departure lounge and my thoughts naturally went to the few hours that lay ahead, where there was I hoped, a completely different climate awaiting me. My hopes were for something a lot drier, warmer and altogether more in keeping with the summer of my dreams.

There was a fairly lengthy delay in boarding the plane; the right transport to assist myself and another wheelchair user had not arrived. This meant that instead of getting on the plane first, which if I remember is the usual practice, all the other passengers boarded ahead of us. All this meant, that when eventually we arrived at the plane and I had been lifted into the tiny chair used to transfer those disabled people needing full assistance and then pushed into the plane proper, there were bodies everywhere. People were milling about sorting out their hand luggage into the lockers over their seats, the cabin crew were helping people and walking up and down the plane and it was a relief to eventually be lifted into my seat and made comfortable by Vee. My first concern once seated, was to make sure that my 'Conveen', a sheath attached to my penis to aid the passing of urine into my leg bag, was still intact. I had been lifted and mauled

9

about four times by this time and the sheath is only stuck to the skin by a thin sticky strip. It would be a disaster if it came away from me, because it would mean that Vee would have to change it with other passengers all around me! A little disconcerting, I imagined, for them to see someone messing about with my private bits! However, once it was ascertained that all was well and that should I need to urinate there would be no problem, then my next concern was to find out that my wheelchair had been properly loaded into the aeroplane. I was assured it had and for the first time that day, I felt a sense of relief wash over me and could began to relax and unwind, to let go of my fears and concerns over the many problems I had envisioned earlier in the day, when my journey had first started.

The first thing I did as I began to settle was to take in my surroundings. I had been so focussed on other things, that I had not felt free enough to look around me and as I did so now, my first thought was how shabby everything looked. I had spent some time prior to the holiday looking on the 'internet', at what was provided by 'British Airways' for 'Club World' passengers and the pictures that appeared on my computer screen, in no way matched up to what I was now looking at. My surroundings looked old, worn and in need of some TLC. There was a lot less space between seats and the aisle was very narrow, only room for one person to walk down, whereas on the photographs I had seen, it appeared that there was a lot more room. The plane itself was quite small and though I knew I wasn't flying in a 'Jumbo Jet', even so, I wondered if this plane was big enough to get to where we were going, a ludicrous though I know, but that was my initial reaction to what I was taking in. By now, I had been sat in my seat for about 30 minutes and my final thought, as movement of the plane signalled the fact that we were soon to take off, was how hard the seat was! Already I was feeling uncomfortable and I knew things were only going to get more uncomfortable, during the next nine hours or so of our flight.

We took off at 5.25 pm, a few minutes late. It was a strange sensation, because I was facing towards the back of the plane, so as the nose lifted up, my balance shifted and I felt myself leaning forward. It was only for a minute or so and once we were flying level, I was able to sort myself out into a reasonably comfortable position again and comforted myself with the thought that it would be much easier for me when it came time to land. Within a very short while the cabin crew began to go about their work, checking on the passengers, tidying up the lockers by putting things away or taking out the likes of spare blankets that had been requested. Then the drinks trolley appeared and I permitted myself the luxury of a glass of champagne. Vee joined me with a glass for herself and we made a toast to the trip. Her seat was next to mine, a window seat, but whereas I was facing to the rear of the plane, she faced towards the front. This meant that we were pretty much facing each other and so could easily converse if we wanted too. I thanked her for her help thus far; noting that she had been calm throughout the journey, helping me with my fears and apprehensions, helping me by reminding me that 'another box had been ticked', as in, another part of the journey had been completed successfully. This was a phrase she said she would use occasionally, to remind me that things were going well. After a chat about the day and about what adventures might possibly come our way, it was time for the in flight meal. Vee is a vegetarian and her meal had been pre booked. I, after looking at the menu card, decided on a salmon starter, followed by beef stroganoff. Another glass of champagne washed it down and even though as a 'Club World' passenger, I could have drank champagne all the way, I decided to be very sensible and sat for the rest of the flight with just a bottle of water.

People all around me, following the meal, were beginning to settle down. Pillows and blankets appeared and the seats were being lowered into their lowest position, that of lying down. Vee asked me if I wanted settling and after making a few adjustments to my seating position, I felt it best not to lay flat for a couple of reasons. One, I can't sleep on my back and there was no way I could be positioned for sleep as I do at home and secondly, I was conscious that having drunk water and juice and champagne, I would before long, be passing water and I wanted to be in a position to control what was happening. I needed to be able to prevent any problems leading to leakage and the need to change my 'Conveen'. This put me in a semi-reclined position, which left me free to check on my water works, free to rest my head, as best I could back onto my pillow and free to avail myself of the in-flight entertainment. This consisted for me, of watching the latest 'Star Trek' movie and then playing chess and backgammon. As I grew more and more tired this became less enjoyable, but try as I might to settle and sleep, there was no-way I could. I was so uncomfortable and I made a conscious decision to sit on my wheelchair cushion, a specialised pressure relief cushion on the return journey home. Looking at my small TV screen and the flight information that you could follow, I noted that it was just gone 10 pm and there was another four hours to go before we were due to land and all I could do, being too uncomfortable to sleep and yet too tired to watch another film or play games, was to think.

I thought once more about how this trip had been made possible and who had made it possible, Kevin and Audrey

James. After the initial contact, made many months previously now, we had kept in touch either via email, which was the easiest way, or on the odd occasion, with a phone call. One of the first things I had asked was why? Why me and why now?

I remembered that one of the first things I did when contact with Kevin had been made, was to try and put a face to the name. I looked through some old photographs I had of my army colleges during my time at the 'Army Physical Training School' based on Queens Avenue in Aldershot, but no Kevin James. Only when they sent some photographs of themselves via email and more information was made available about that time, did I realise that in reality, whilst we were both at Aldershot in 1981, we were in fact going through the process of transferring, via the course, into the 'Army Physical Training Corp', (A.P.T.C.) at different times, we were in different intakes. At the time of my accident, I was at the stage of 'Junior Probationers' and Kevin was an intake behind me doing the 'Advanced Course'. So, whilst I may have seen Kevin around the school, we would not have spent any time together, because we were separated by our different stages of the transfer to the 'Corp' and so would not in all honesty remember him.

As part of being at the school, anyone with any gymnastic ability was recruited into the school display team. I was not great at gymnastics, having started so late in life in gymnastic terms. It's a sport you have to take up in your early teens or younger, to properly develop the skills of balance, suppleness, spatial awareness and strength to perform the routines involved in gymnastics. I came into the sport here at the school for the first time aged 25 and whilst I certainly had the physical strength, I had very little spatial awareness and managed to get through the routines through repetition, teaching the muscles of my body what to do and when to do it. Still, I was good enough to be on the team, as was Kevin and this was our link. He told me in one phone conversation, that on the day of my accident, at one part of the show, he had been right behind me in the routine and as I ran to perform my trick over the vaulting horse, he was barely a second or so behind me. Apparently he went on to say, the guy in front of me was quite a heavy built man and he had jumped on the spring board, a fibreglass board used to help propel us over the vaulting horse, with some force and as I landed on it, it was still recovering from the previous use and so gave me an extra lift, taking me higher than I had intended to go. This caused me to over-rotate leading me to land head first and not feet first and so resulting in my breaking my neck. He had seen all this and had thankfully managed to avoid landing on me and his reason for thinking about me all these years and for wanting to make contact with me after watching the TV programme was, he said, that it could easily have been him. Due to some illnesses or injuries in the display team that Saturday, there had been some changes of position within the three groups that made up the team and he could quite easily have been where I was and may well have ended up in my position, flat out on the safety mat with a broken neck. As Kevin put it, "there but for the grace of God go I". That one thought had been with him, with both Kevin and Audrey for all the intervening years and after seeing the programme, they had felt it right to make a concerted effort to make contact. It took them a while to track me down they said, but eventually they found me and one thing led to another, to another, to even a visit to my home from Kevin who was over for a few days early in 2009, visiting family and friends. I learnt so much from him during that time, about his past and present life, to what he saw of my accident, to the basic plans for my time with them later in the year. All of that led me to being sat on this aeroplane, heading towards the sun, sea and sand. So that was the answer to my questions of why me and why now and as a committed Christian, I prayed, whilst thirty five thousand feet or so in the air, a simple prayer of thanks, for making all that was going to happen in the next fourteen days possible.

Apart from the little I did know about the holiday, what few plans and thoughts of how our time was to be spent initially, the remainder of our time on the island, an island called Soldier (Cay), pronounced key, was a mystery. So what did I know? What had been planned thus far? Well, money had been kindly sent by Kevin and Audrey to pay for one flight ticket, I had then paid the extra for Vee's ticket and the upgrade for us both. We were now en-route to Nassau, the capital of the Bahamas, where Kevin should be waiting to drive us to 'Paradise Island' where we would be staying in a luxury resort called 'Atlantis' on the edge of the capital. We would be staying in one of the chain of hotels there called 'Beach Towers' for three nights, again paid for by Kevin and Audrey, for three reasons. One, to acclimatise to the weather, two, to do the touristy bit of the holiday and to meet some of their friends who house sit for them in Nassau and three, to give them both time to finish off whatever final preparations were needed on Soldier Cay, in order to make our stay as comfortable as they had promised it would be. The plan was, that Kevin would stay near bye and show us around for the first day. Then, they would swap over and Audrey would take us around some of the shops and introduce us to their friends and then help us on the final two-part section of the journey to their island. A two-part journey, because the island being so small, only 4 acres or so, there is no-where for the small private plane we would be using to land. So, we would be flying to a bigger island further up the group that make up the Exuma Chain and then from there, by boat to Soldier Cay. All in all, quite a trip, with what for me appeared, as yet, more obstacles to overcome and more 'boxes to be ticked' and this all before we even arrive on the island we would be staying at for the remainder of the holiday. Still, nothing ventured nothing gained was the expression that jumped to my mind, as I sat with my ever increasing numb bottom, drawing closer and closer to the end of what was for me, my first ever long haul flight.

At around 2 am, the cabin crew were once again becoming more active, as lights were turned on and again lockers were being opened and closed. Drinks were brought and then warm face cloths handed out, to help refresh our tired faces.

We landed at Nassau without any problems, certainly not for me anyway. This was due mostly to the fact that, as I was facing the rear of the plane, my body weight was being pushed, under breaking, into the back of my seat. This made it easier and more comfortable to cope with than the take off had been. We were then informed over the tannoy, that the local time was 9.25 pm. But my body clock was reminding me that it was actually 2.25 am and oh boy didn't I know that. Once the plane was stationary, then begun yet another wait for the assistance I needed to get off and through all the checks and baggage collection. This took quite a while which was frustrating, but one of the cabin crew warned me, that things move at a greatly reduced speed over here in the Bahamas and that it was something I would have to get used too during my stay. The plane soon emptied of passengers, leaving only a few of the cabin crew, the cleaning detail that had arrived to clear the debris away and to prepare the plane for it's next journey, Vee and myself.

When eventually somebody did arrive, I was once again lifted from my seat into the chair used to negotiate the narrow aisle. From that chair, just outside the plane, I was transferred into a standard wheelchair and someone started pushing me away from the plane towards the terminal. During the polite conversation between the three of us, as we walked the once again huge distance between plane and terminal, one of the first things that struck me, was the almost oppressive heat. Bearing in mind that it was closing in on 9.55 pm local time, the temperature, or at least the humidity, was extremely high. I love the heat, I love the feeling of being warmed by the sun, but this was akin to walking into a sauna, something else I have only had the pleasure of once. I shuddered at the thought of trying to get to sleep in these conditions, but remembered as I thought that, that air-conditioning was standard pretty much everywhere you went, certainly in this neck of the woods. Another thing to strike me, was the thought that my red chair would be no-where in sight, but the first thing I did see, upon reaching the arrivals section of the terminal, was my chair looking pretty much as I had left it, no missing parts and nothing bent or out of place and within a few seconds, extra hands had been mustered and I was safely transferred, at last sitting on my own cushion, much to the relief of my bottom.

Our baggage had been labelled at Heathrow so that it would be amongst the first to be brought through to baggage claim. It therefore only took us a few seconds to retrieve our bags and once again get assistance to the front of the queue at customs, for the final part of the arrivals process. A minute or so later, having been given back our passports, we headed off to the arrivals lounge where Kevin, with a welcoming smile, was on hand to greet us and take charge of our last leg of our inbound journey. It was great to finally meet up with him and tired as I was, I never the less enjoyed telling him all about our journey thus far. Kevin is a strong individual and very easily lifted me into the passenger seat of his car. Once the chair and luggage had been stowed away in the boot, he drove us the twenty minutes or so it took to get to the 'Atlantis' resort, where we would be staying for the first three nights.

The main reception desk was closed at this time of night and we had to walk several hundred yards to a second desk to check in and then back again. It was therefore, 11.10 pm local time, 4.10 am to me, when we finally walked into my room at the 'Beach Tower' hotel. We made a quick plan for the morning, very much dependant on what time we were up and about and after a long cool drink, Vee somehow managed to get me onto the bed. I say somehow, because it was a huge bed, wide and high. The top of the mattress must have been at least six inches above the height of my wheelchair cushion. So, where normally at home, my transfer from chair to bed is level and simply a matter of sliding straight across, here I had the problem of going up as well as across. After a quick thought, we decided that I would firstly put my feet onto the mattress, then, roll my upper body onto the bed with Vee pushing my hips, ensuring that I was fully on the bed. The position I finally ended up in was a little ungainly, but at least I was safely on. After being straightened out flat on my back, I was undressed and then discovered that, after worrying all day that my 'Conveen' might come off due to the lifts and transfers, but had survived so far, had indeed just come off, because of the method employed in getting me onto the bed.

Still, I was on the bed, not in a taxi or plane and so cleaning me, changing the 'Conveen' for a fresh one, was not a major problem. Within a few minutes I was ready to sleep, with what is so typical for me, after all that had been so positive about the day, a worry in my head that I had not brought enough 'Conveens' with me? I had packed ten for the two weeks and I had used one after the first day, would there be enough I thought?

Day 2.

The worry over the 'Conveen' count must have been my final thought for the night, for the next thing I can remember, is waking up with a little light showing through the bedroom curtains and Vee trying to close the door as quietly as possible as she made her way in. Realising I was awake, started off a conversation between us about how well or not we had slept and a question from Vee, asking if I was ready to get up? I asked what the time was and was very surprised when she said that it was 7.20 am. My mind again made a quick calculation about the time difference and I realised that the time back home was 12.20 pm. I had slept for eight hours without waking, a rare thing for me, but under the present circumstances, a pleasant realisation. I then made a silent promise to myself, to stop figuring out what time it was back home, I was in the Bahamas now and my body clock would get used to the idea quicker, I thought, if I stopped reminding myself about the time difference.

I did indeed want to get up; I have never been one for lazy mornings in bed and if the day has started and the sun is shining, then I have always wanted to be a part of it. I remember many years ago, when my wife, Ilona, was my main carer before we started using social services. I woke up one morning and because she preferred to sleep with the window slightly open and the curtains drawn back, just enough to let a little light in, it meant that the room was full of the sound of birds singing and lit up by the morning summer sun. I had slept well and so wanted to get up straight away. I called Ilona's name softly till she woke and after turning towards me, she asked if all was well. I told her that I was ready to get up, but, after checking her bedside clock and informing me that it was only 5.00 am, turned over and went back to sleep, leaving me to lie there for several more hours until she was ready herself to get me up. A throw back in all likelihood, to my early mornings in the army.

Vee had been to my house a couple of times prior to us leaving; she had come with Val to see how to get me into and out of bed. She knew therefore, just about, my routine for the morning and soon my lower half was dressed, as it would be for the duration of our stay in Nassau, in lightweight trousers and slip on shoes and I was sitting in my chair. Vee then drew back the curtains and gasped wow! I pushed myself to the window to check on the view for myself and had a very similar reaction to her. The view was awesome. We were on the fifth floor of the hotel and from where I was sitting I could see on my right the ocean, the beach and the palm trees. Then, coming more centrally in front of my room, the pools and sunbathing areas that dotted around the hotel complex. I could see in the near distance a series of pools with turtles and other marine life swimming around in them and in the far distance the other hotels that made up the 'Atlantis' resort. The sky had a few light puffy clouds, but there appeared to be no wind. The sea was a colour I had never seen in any water around Britain to my knowledge; it truly was an awesome sight.

The plan, as quickly formulated the night before, was to phone Kevin, who would then meet us in my room and be our guide for that day, before flying back to the island leaving us with Audrey for the remainder of the time in Nassau. So, after a wash and a shave and having my top half clothed with a tee shirt, this we did. Twenty minutes later, Kevin joined us and after the usual pleasantries about sleeping well enough, we made our way down to the ground floor to seek out the dining area for breakfast.

I have often heard that pretty much everything overseas is twice the size of that found in the UK. Well the Atlantis resort, made up of several hotels all linked together by a covered walkway, come shopping centre, with conference facilities, restaurants and the odd fountain or two along the route we were taking, was proving that point exactly. It was enormous. We had been walking for about five minutes and were still no-where near the breakfast bar. It took us a further two minutes to walk through the casino, which to my amazement already had guests putting coins into the rows and rows of slot machines that made up the majority of the floor space. Eventually we reached the American style buffet breakfast bar and even though there was a queue waiting to get in, Kevin took charge of the situation and within a minute we had bypassed the queue and were being shown to a table. Walking up to the food area was another eye opener for me. It was full of every imaginable food type you could think of. The bar went on and on and after completing the circuit once, looking over all of the delicacies and catching so many different aromas from the variety of food that was being cooked right in front of you, I struggled to come up with a choice and being ever so British, I plumped for a plate of sausage, beans and scrambled eggs! Pathetic! Still, this I figured was to be my first and only breakfast during my stay in the Bahamas. I've never been a big fan of breakfasts since my accident, I feel my system needed time to settle after a nights sleep and I have struggled since to face up to food first thing in the morning, unless that is, I'm in a hotel where I have paid for the meal as part of the cost of the stay, then I would force myself to eat something! The up side to having breakfast here today was the entertainment. There wasn't any show going on as such, but using the dining room, as well as the paying guests, were the contestants for the forthcoming 'Miss Universe' contest. They were tall, slender and in the main, quite pretty girls, surrounded by bodyguards and were being constantly photographed by cameramen and guests alike. Whether they were there for the food was doubtful, most of them looked like they needed a good meal, but no-doubt had more on their mind than food at that time.

Once we had finished our meal, Kevin took us on a tour of the complex. Everywhere indoors had air conditioning and so it was cool, but once we stepped outside, ouch! Once again I felt as though we were stepping into a sauna. It was only 10.30 am and already as hot as I had ever felt it back home, only this was humid as well as hot and whilst I enjoyed the feeling, compared to the cool indoor environment, after a while, even I was glad of a walk through the aquarium, where we could view the many exotic fish on show through the thick glass that surrounded us. There were large and small varieties and amazing to see at such close a distance. We wandered around the pools I had first seen from my bedroom window earlier this morning. Walked past the marina that berthed several yachts, the size of which my home would comfortably fit in, they must have been worth millions. We wandered past some shops where we bought bottled water and at one of the few kiosks that sold little trinkets and souvenirs, I put my hand into my pocket for the first of only three occasions during the holiday, where I spent any of my own money, apart that is from paying the extra for the flights and the travel to the airport and bought a key ring for Dieter, a friend of mine back home.

I had known Dieter Eggebrecht for many years. In fact I first met him in 1986, during my first stay at the Worthing ex-servicemen's hospital home I went to for the respite break I took and have continued to take ever since. He was one of the care staff that looked after the men who, either lived at the home full time, or, like me, visited for a short break. We had hit it off straight away. I'm a few years older than he is, but we were otherwise so similar with regard to humour and likes. We would take shopping trips together, then visits to the local pub and gradually over the years, spend time on his off days, either at his home with his wife Penny, or out enjoying the local tourist sites where he would graciously push my chair over all manner of terrain. At my last visit to their home, I had been talking about my forthcoming trip abroad and Dieter had mentioned that, for many years, he had been collecting key rings as a hobby. He asked if I wouldn't mind picking him up something local to the Bahamas, so that he could add to his collection and that was precisely what I did. Of the many that were for sale, I chose one that was fashioned to look like a flip-flop and with the word Bahamas clearly visible on it's sole. Several weeks later, after my holiday, I presented it to him and he was very pleased with it and was happy to add it to his number.

At 1.30 pm, Kevin left us to get back to Soldier Cay. He told us that Audrey would meet us in the hotel lobby around 5.30 pm, the plan being that she and I would be going out for a meal to a local restaurant, giving Vee some time to herself. Vee and I then spent the rest of the afternoon wandering around outside where we bought some lunch, rather cheekily charging it to my room. It was still incredibly hot, so we found some shade where we could eat in comfort. Once our lunch was finished, we wandered to the beach and after sitting and watching the Jet Ski's buzzing about on the sea for a few minutes, we headed back to the hotel to cool down, wash and then change for the evening.

During all the preparations for this trip, I had been in regular contact via emails with Kevin and Audrey, although I suspect it was Audrey who wrote most of the messages. As well as the information about all the arrangements being made, there was some time given in the messages to reminiscing about the past, to Aldershot and the day of my accident. It had taken a while, but I had gotten used to having the vague memory of Kevin being at the school the same time as me, even though, apart from the display's we were giving, we otherwise spent no time at all together. Now, as these conversations via email were going on, Audrey was telling me that she too, as Kevin's wife, had been at the show that fateful day of July 11th and had witnessed my accident. She went on further to say that, just prior to our show, I had given her my baseball cap to keep safe for me, a memory long since lost to me. She wrote often about how she had a pretty good memory of my personality and me, even if I had no memory of her and she was looking forward to catching up after all these years. So, meeting with her in the lobby of the hotel later, would be interesting on many fronts.

Vee and I arrived at the lobby around 5.15 and found a comfortable spot to sit and wait that gave us a good view of the hotel entrance. We chatted about our time there so far, Vee reminding me of the many boxes we had ticked off already and of the fact that nothing had gone wrong so far, a fact that wasn't lost to me. The smiling face of Audrey coming towards us interrupted our conversation; they had sent several photographs of them on their island, so recognising her was not an issue. She gave me a hug and a kiss on the cheek, saying how good it was to finally meet up. I then introduced her to Vee and they greeted each other warmly. Audrey then sat down with us and we chatted about what we had been doing through the day. The conversation quickly moved on to the plan for the evening, it being that Audrey was taking me to a local restaurant so that we could catch up more, leaving Vee to herself, giving her the opportunity to explore the complex further and to have a rest from caring for me. That being agreed, they between them got me into Audrey's car and with a word or two about roughly what time we should be back at the hotel, we drove off.

After a ten-minute drive, we ended up outside the entrance to 'Luciano's' restaurant where, after assembling the wheelchair, Audrey gathered a couple of the restaurant staff to help me up the six or seven steps to the main entrance. She was obviously a regular diner at 'Luciano's', as she knew by name a couple of the staff, as well as some of the other patrons who were there for the night out.

We were shown to our table which was right on the sea front giving us a fantastic view of the bay. I could see the back of the hotels making up the 'Atlantis' resort in the far distance and with the coloured lights that adorned the trestelling around the outside dining area and the cooling and welcome sea breeze, it really was a picture you only see in the movies. The menu I was handed was full of food I had never heard of. Local fish delicacies and spices not known to me and certainly not to be found in my nearby shops in and around Borrowash and so I left it to Audrey to choose. I ended up eating a Conch fritter to start, followed by shrimp and asparagus tips on a bed of rice, washed down with a glass of red wine. The whole evening was a delight and although in truth I wasn't that hungry, due to the heat and having had breakfast and lunch already that day, it never the less was a great time. We chatted about all sorts of things, from our past, our careers and aspirations, to what sort of things we both did and enjoyed doing day to day. It was getting late and darkness meant that our view from our dining table had changed slightly. The coloured lights that were hanging all around us were brighter and we could see lights bobbing about on the water, either from moored boats or those that were going about the bay full of tourists. The hotels across the bay were now dark shapes, but their outside lights meant you could easily make out the different individual buildings. A short sharp shower interrupted our enjoyment of the view and we, as did the other patrons sitting outside under the stars, dashed for cover for the few minutes it took for the squall to pass. Audrey organised one of the waiters to take some snapshots of us at our table and then we headed back to my hotel. It was about 11.00 pm and I was getting more and more tired by the minute. The events of the day, the heat and all the food I had consumed were taking its toll on me and as we drove back, a little more subdued than when we had driven out, I made a promise to myself to eat a lot less in the remaining days, than I had this day!

As we pulled up outside the hotel, Vee was there already, enjoying the evening air and it wasn't long before I was back in my chair and after once again making plans for the following day, only this time with Audrey, Vee pushed me off to my room and helped me onto the toilet, a blessed relief to my aching stomach! I then got into bed, after first of all loosening the straps that holds the leg bag around my calf, so that the manoeuvre of climbing onto the high mattress didn't pull on the 'Conveen', as it did the first night. Once more I was asleep before too long, after quickly reflecting on an extraordinary day, the first full day in the Bahamas.

Day 3.

A faint noise woke me up. Vee was moving about in the room and after letting her know I was awake, I found out from her that it was just gone 9.30 am! An unusually late morning for me, although not surprising considering how tired I had been last night. Vee told me that she had come into my room around the same time as yesterday, but upon realising I was sound asleep, left me as I was and just sat reading her book. Getting up was the same routine as yesterday, as it is for everyday for me. Doing things like going to bed and getting dressed rarely differ, apart from what clothes I'm wearing, that way it keeps it simple and quicker to do. We decided not to venture out of the room for breakfast, it had been a long walk yesterday and so Vee ordered from room service. She ordered for herself, a bowl of mixed fruit and some orange juice and I just had some juice and hot water from the kettle in the room. I had stopped drinking tea and coffee over twenty years ago, preferring instead the simple taste of hot water and the simplicity in its making. I was told it was good for the digestion and all manner of other health reasons, but I'm happy in the knowledge that I can make myself a hot drink, as quickly as it takes to boil a kettle. The only variance is in the taste and quality of water and whilst we were advised not to drink cold water from the tap over here, boiled water presented no problems. A knock at the door a few minutes after phoning our order signalled breakfast had arrived and twenty minutes or so later, we were heading down and out of the hotel for a walk around outside, for some fresh air. We stuck with the route we knew, again going through the maze of underground passages that made up the aquarium, then strolled around the hotel complex out in the sun.

We had agreed to meet with Audrey where we had met last night, in the hotel lobby at around 11.45 am and this we did. After a quick chat about our respective mornings, we headed off for lunch. Audrey was taking us to a local bar away from the complex, giving us a feel for the real Bahamas and not the contrived one you get from a purpose built holiday site, which was the 'Atlantis' resort.

After a fifteen-minute stroll, we ended up at a bar called the 'Green Parrot'. It was right on the waterfront and was very much out in the open, apart that is from the central bar situated under a roof on stilts. Under the roof, as well as the bar, were a few tables dotted about for guests and then an outside patio area, with tables under shady trees or in the sunshine. We chose a table under a tree, to keep out of the midday heat, but also to enjoy the view of the ocean and to catch what cooling breeze there was. I love the sun, but I had become quickly aware of just how intense it was at this time of day and as I wasn't sunbathing, in the proper sense, I agreed that the shelter the tree afforded was spot on to fully enjoy our meal and our time together. Where we were sitting gave us an excellent view of the harbour, the harbour where the luxury liners that brought the tourists berthed. The weekend, according to Audrey, was an especially busy time for these huge boats to come into the anchorage, mainly from Florida. They would stop over for a night or so, giving the passengers on board, who were either on a long cruise, or those on a weekend trip, ample time to spend their money at the casino of the complex, or one of the many shops selling their overpriced wares. This being a Saturday meant that the harbour was fast filling up with these boats and others we could see in the far distance who were waiting their turn to come in. Nearer to where we were sitting, were barge type boats that Audrey called the 'mail boats'. She told us that the government of the Bahamas is obliged to supply an inter island mail service and the boats that were commissioned to carry the mail between the islands became known simply as mail boats. Now though, even though they carry all manner of freight, vehicles, supplies, people etc, they retain that name. So for instance, if Kevin and Audrey needed anything specific for Soldier Cay, whereas you or I would jump in our car and drive to the shops to buy our food items or new fridge freezer, they, being on a remote island many miles away from the nearest shop, would make a phone call to the main island of Nassau and then one of the boats we were currently looking at, would drop those goods off. All that of course was dependant upon the weather and the state of the seas, so planning ahead for all eventualities was part of their life as managers of the island.

Audrey, as she had done the night before took charge of the menu, ordering a simple lunch of fabulous tasting coconut shrimp, a variety of fish fritters, all locally caught, the fish that is, fries, onion rings and an assortment of dips. We washed all this down with a few bottles of the local beer called 'Kalik'. So called, Audrey reliably informed us, because of the sound two bottles make when knocked together as you make a toast, or when greeting a fellow drinker! A nice thought whether true or not. Either way, the beer tasted good, as did the food and the two hours or so we were there passed away in a very enjoyable manner. We spent the time with more catching up between Audrey and myself and it also gave an opportunity for Vee to share for the first time with Audrey a bit about herself, giving her a more rounded picture of who my carer was.

Lunch over; we strolled back in the direction of our hotel, stopping off on the way at some shops. This was to be our last opportunity to buy gifts for friends and family back home, so I took advantage of that and bought a couple of clothing items for my wife. One was a colourful sarong type wrap and then a long sleeveless tee shirt that can be worn either as a nightshirt, a day sundress, or something you could put on by the pool after a swim. Again, it too was brightly coloured with the words Bahamas and Nassau on it and small pictures of turtles and seaweed on the pockets. Gifts that I knew, as soon as I saw them, Ilona would love. We finally made it back to our hotel around 3.00 pm, where, I was able to cool off near the air conditioning vent in my room and put my feet up on a chair for a few minutes before starting the afternoon's surprise entertainment!

It was not really a surprise, because prior to coming over, Kevin had asked if I would like to have a swim with dolphins! Apparently over on the far side of the complex there was a dolphin marina, or 'Dolphin Cay' as it was advertised. Guests of the hotel could swim with and be entertained by the dolphins and it was drawing close to my turn to have a go. Vee gave me a helping hand to put my swimming shorts on, then my trousers over them. We again met up with Audrey who took us on what seemed like a five-mile trek; only it wasn't, to where the marina was sited. After booking in, we had a short wait in an area where you could sit and see the large pool the dolphins were in, going through their routines with the other guests before us. After a few more minutes we were taken to the changing areas where, with some difficulty, I was squeezed into a wet suit. I was then transferred onto a chair especially made for disabled guests. One that can only be described as a plastic patio chair with four large balloon like tyres, as in the 'Monster Trucks' the Americans love to drive over rows of wrecked cars, only not as big obviously. The large wheels were to help get across the beach that fronted the pool, leading to where the dolphins swam. There were about twenty other guests with me and after viewing a short video all about dolphins, we were taken outside and split into two teams.

Now, I can't recall the last time I swam in any body of water, pool, or the ocean. It was certainly something I did as part of my rehab, swimming in a pool whilst lying on my back, flotation aids around me, flinging my arms behind me and pulling them through under my shoulders to propel me backwards. That must have been around the early eighties, shortly after my accident and apart from the occasional workout in the hydrotherapy pool the hospital home I go to in Worthing used to have, I have not properly swam since then. Swimming in the ocean or a pool prior to my accident, you can go back even further to the mid to late seventies, when I was still having holidays with my family, or visiting the Lido in Uttoxeter where I lived. So, at the time of writing this, nearly thirty years have passed since I was properly wet, apart that is, from a bath or a shower!

I have always been ok about being in water, as long as it's not too cold, although I'm not one of those naturally gifted swimmers. I developed and grew, through my exercise regime, to be heavy boned and very muscular, elements that make floating rather difficult. I remember going through a swimming course whilst at Aldershot, just prior to breaking my neck. We were told to line up in the pool, shortest in the shallow end and the taller guys heading off to the deep end, so that the water came level with the top of our shoulders. We were then told to take a breath and curl up into a ball and wait for a whistle before standing upright again. Having done what I was told, I can clearly remember opening my eyes after feeling my toes touch the bottom of the pool and looking around me, I noticed that I was not the only person bobbing about at the bottom of the pool. There were three or four others with me who were also glancing around. After hearing the whistle, the instructor informed those of us that sank, that our body mass was such that we were sinkers and not floaters, and so, whilst being able to swim, were not the natural swimmers that did rather well in the pool sports. A sentiment I whole-heartedly agreed with. I was always the one at the pool who dived or jumped in, splashed about a bit, but spent most of the time sunbathing and because of my physique, posing!

So now, I'm just about ready to go into the pool with the dolphins, wondering how cold the water is, how am I going to stay stable and upright in the water. My mind initially was all over the place, giving very little thought to the fact that I'm just about to go swimming with dolphins, an experience many people would jump at the chance to do, given the opportunity I now have.

A staff member has been assigned to assist me and after we have all had our final instructions about what we should and shouldn't do in the pool, we head off. Audrey and Vee are behind me giving me words of encouragement and Audrey is also busy with her camera, taking snap shots of this occasion and indeed the rest of the holiday, photos I have come to treasure. Now the chair, as I have mentioned, is especially designed to cope with the soft sand thanks to its balloon tyres, however, once it reaches the water things are very different. It soon becomes unstable and my carer has real difficulty in keeping the chair upright. He eventually calls for help and I'm lifted out of the chair and carried to the deeper part of the pool, where the rest of the team I'm in are and where the dolphins will come too in order for us to interact with them. Once I begin to feel reassured that no one is going to drop me, the next thing I notice is the temperature of the water. My paralysis means that I can only feel heat or the cold in a small part of my body. This is primarily my face, neck, shoulders and part of my arms and hands and once these parts are deep enough in the pool, I notice that, whilst not hydrotherapy pool temperature, it's rather pleasant and my fears of getting cold are allayed.

With my carer holding me in a comfortable position, both for him and me, the dolphins were released from one end of the quite large pool and one is assigned to each of the two teams. The team I'm in are told that our dolphins name is Isis and that it's a female of about three years of age. It then went through a series of tricks and poses, swimming close to each of us in the team, allowing us to touch it's back or belly, to feed it with a fish and also allowing us to kiss it, not that pleasant a sensation, but something that was obviously part of the routine. After about fifteen minutes, the two teams join up and the two dolphins did a series of leaps and twists to order out in the deeper water. It was a fabulous sight, but I have to admit that by this point, I was beginning to feel cold and was more concerned about getting out of the water to get warm and back into my chair to get comfortable.

This done, we were then shepherded through the gift shop, the only way out back to the hotel complex. Audrey kindly bought some souvenir photographs of my time in the pool, which had been taken by another staff member, whose job it was to snap each guest with the dolphin for this very purpose.

It took some considerable time to get through the queue of guests buying their chosen photographs and I so desperately wanted to go outside into the sunshine to get warm and the longer it took, the more agitated I became. Nevertheless, my overriding memory of that time was of how unique an experience it had been, something I had never thought possible, for me anyway. It really opened my eyes to what can be achieved, regardless of disability and I would hear myself saying that phrase to myself more and more in the following days. Once outside, I did quickly warm up and after a gentle stroll, we headed back to my room where I got changed for the evening.

At around 5.30 pm, we once again all met up in the lobby, ready for the short walk that Audrey had told us would be all that was needed to reach her main island home here in Nassau. They had taken the opportunity to buy this home in case there was ever a need to be off Soldier Cay and for any future needs they may have. For the time being, two very good friends of theirs, Roy and Marilyn, were house sitting for them. They had been living there for a few years now, taking care of things and when we arrived became instant friends to us both. They hailed from Sheffield, were down to earth folk and very friendly. When we entered the living room, the first thing Vee noticed was that Roy was watching English football and the results from today's fixtures. She, being an ardent Leeds United FC fan, had an instant connection with him and they were, within seconds, both chatting away about football and their respective teams.

I'm not such a big fan of football as Vee and certainly not whilst in company. So Audrey, Marilyn and I, contended ourselves with a cool drink and a chat, where I shared the story of my life and everything that lead to my being here in the Bahamas. We had a meal of pasta and fish, as in all types of fish, an ice cream dessert and a couple of glasses of wine. After the meal we sat outside and admired Audrey's pride and joy, her garden. She told us of all the plans she had for it and of how hard it had been to get it looking a well as it did today. Two hours of relaxing conversation later, I had a sense of being tired, which was not surprising considering the day I had had and after making fresh plans with Audrey for the next day, Sunday, we thanked Roy and Marilyn for the wonderful evening, wished them all a good night and Vee and I set off on our own, back to the hotel. It had been a straight and simple route in getting there and apart from the minor swerves due to the wine; it was a straight and easy road back. After again being helped onto the toilet, I was soon in bed and once more reflecting on all that I had done. The lovely meal at the 'Green Parrot', the swim with Isis the dolphin and to cap it all, the meal and company of Roy and Marilyn, another great day.

Day 4.

Sunday the 9th of August started bright and early and I was pretty much dressed and in my chair by around 8.00 am. Vee had packed her bag ready for the trip over to Soldier Cay and had brought it to my room so that when we were ready to go, everything would be in one place and to hand. She once more ordered breakfast from room service and once that was out of the way, we packed up most of my things. We weren't due to meet Audrey until around 12.30 pm, she had plans in town, last minute shopping and other arrangements to make before leaving Nassau, so the morning was ours.

We had noticed on our long trek to the dolphin cay yesterday, an area where there was a water ride, a slalom called 'The Lazy River', where you sat in an inflated plastic ring and were taken around by the flow of water. There were other water entertainments in the same location that guests could enjoy and Vee had expressed an interest in having a go, so that was where we were heading. We got there easily enough and found that the ride opened at 10.00 am and in the few minutes remaining before the ride started, I found myself a quiet spot that gave me a good view of part of the river. Then, whilst facing the already hot morning sun, I took off my tee shirt and actually sun bathed for the first time since arriving. There soon followed a flurry of activity, as guests began to get into the river, having noticed that the water was now flowing and after Vee chose her ring to sit in, she joined them and with a smile on her face, drifted off out of my sight. I had no idea how long the ride was going to take, but where I sat I could see both the beginning of the river and the end, so I knew that eventually, Vee would reappear around the bend ahead of me. I lost myself in topping up what suntan I already had from home, turning my chair every few minutes so that the sun was first on my back, or as much of my back that was visible above the back of the wheelchair and then my front. I had a bottle of water with me and a packet of crisps we had bought the day before, but never got around to eating and this was all I intended to have until we arrived in Soldier Cay later today. I also passed the time by people watching. We humans are a diverse lot and I have always been fascinated by how people interact with each other, or by how they behave in groups, or on their own and I was seeing some real diversity as I watched the people around me.

Suddenly, Vee was walking towards me; I had missed her finishing off her ride. She dried and told me all about it, sharing how in some parts the water was flowing quite quickly and gave the ride that extra kick. Then it slowed and meandered around in shallower water, giving you the opportunity, should you wish, to get off at different points of the river as it snaked through the area that made up the water entertainment. I put my tee shirt back on and we headed back to the hotel, first stopping at one of the complex's swimming pools, allowing Vee the chance to have one last splash. I tried to find some shade because it was now midday and it was really hot. It was made worse for me, due to the fact that there was very little breeze about. The large brick buildings making up the Atlantis complex, absorbed and reflected out the suns heat, as well as blocking off any sea breeze that was about. So, no matter where I sat in the shade, the heat was unbearable for me and I was glad when Vee eventually returned and we could enter the hotel complex and the coolness offered by its air conditioning.

Once back in my room, I took in plenty of cooling liquids, had a cold wash and then finished off the final few bits of packing. At 12.30 pm we were once again in the hotel lobby where Audrey met us, checked us out and paid the bill. She then helped us outside with our bags and walking ahead of us, began to make her way towards, what she had simply described in the hotel, as our transport to the airport. It was actually a white stretch limousine!

It wasn't the easiest of vehicles to get into for me, but between the two of them, one pulling one pushing, Vee and Audrey got me in. I was then followed by whatever baggage couldn't fit into the boot, because of the size and shape of the wheelchair, which was taking up so much space. These stretch limousines look great and I have to admit, it was fun to ride in one, yet another first for me on this trip, but in terms of being practical for luggage and shopping, not ideal. However, after a few minutes of swapping things around between the boot and the cabin space in between our feet, the driver eventually closed the doors and off we went.

We were heading off to the section of the airport at Nassau where the private planes came and went, stopping off on the way for some fuel for the car. We also stopped because Audrey noticed a street vendor selling fresh mangos and she popped out and bought a few. Once at the airport, the process of unloading all our baggage started and at some point in all of that, I was informed that one of my brakes, the one for the right hand wheel, to be precise, had come off! Having efficient brakes is essential for all vehicles and it's no different for a wheelchair. In order to transfer successfully and safely, the brakes have to be applied and be firm enough to prevent the chair from moving away from where ever it is you are trying to get out of, into or onto. This for me was devastating news and it was only when I was reassured that nothing had actually broken, only come loose, although I don't know how, unless it was during the process of trying to get it into the boot of the limo, and then I had been told that all the bits necessary to put it back on, nuts and bolts etc, were complete and not lost, did I calm down. Audrey did her level best to assure me, that Kevin would have no bother in putting it all back together again. With that, after being carefully lifted into my chair, because of the brake issue, we made our way into the airport waiting area to await our pilot and small private plane we would be using to fly to Staniel Cay, one of only a few islands that make up the Exuma chain of islands that has an airstrip.

We were eventually united with our pilot, obviously a friend of Audrey, who then, after greeting Vee and myself, escorted us out to the plane. The plane was a six-seater and for the life of me, I had no idea as to how I was going to get aboard. All became very clear moments later, when Audrey began to explain to the pilot and another gentleman that Audrey had asked for help from, how things were going to be done. It was obvious that Kevin and Audrey had given this some thought prior to my arriving and from what she was saying, it made sense and seemed pretty much the only way for me to get in. The plan was, that my chair was to be parked next to the rear of the wing, on the side of the right front passenger door. I would then be picked up, turned so that I was facing the tail of the plane and sat on the wing with someone already up there to hold and support me. Then as someone pushed from the ground, the person behind would grab hold of my trouser waistband and drag me up the wing backwards to the door! Then I was to be posted in, still backwards, through the door and positioned on one of the seats in the middle row. Once everyone knew what they were doing, they all set too and remarkably, within a couple of minutes I was sitting in my seat. I have to say, that of all the transfers I have done since breaking my neck, that was the most bizarre and yet simplest. It was however, not the most comfortable transfer. For, as well as having my bottom dragged up the wing and anyone with potential pressure sore problems would tell you, that dragging fragile skin over a rough surface is highly to be avoided, by the time I was in my seat, my trousers felt as though they were disappearing up my bottom! When eventually Vee was able to board, the first thing I asked of her, was to pull my trouser legs down to alleviate the discomfort and then to quickly check on my 'Conveen', to make sure that after all that mauling, things were still intact. Thankfully all was well and a few minutes later, at around 2.30 pm, we were taking off and with the Atlantis complex fast disappearing; we headed off to Staniel Cay and our rendezvous with Kevin.

Our flying time was to be approximately thirty minutes and thanks to the clear skies that seemed, to me anyway, a permanent facet of this location, the views below me were awesome. From my seat I could see clearly the planes instrument panel and the altimeter showed, once we had levelled off, that we were flying at a little under two thousand feet, which meant the view of the ocean below was clear and uninterrupted. I was struck mainly by the colours of the water. They ranged from the palest of blue, to turquoise. There were such a variety and range of colours, colours I had never seen before. Normally, when describing the sea, certainly around most of the British Isles, you would use mucky brown or dark green, never the colours I was seeing now. I could also see the changing depth of the water, indicated by the white sand being visible or the coral and seaweed, then the darker blues. There were rocky outcrops and then gradually, the chain of islands known as the Exuma chain came into view. After twenty minutes or so, Audrey turned to me and pointed to her left, saying that Soldier Cay was coming up, unfortunately, from where I was sitting it wasn't visible, but it all pointed to the fact that we were almost there and I had a real sense that the holiday proper was soon to begin.

I was right, ten minutes later the pilot began to make small adjustments on his instrument panel and I noticed that the altimeter was slowly decreasing in numbers. We were on a slow descent and after a few more minutes, Staniel Cay came into view. The pilot took the plane in a slow turn around the island and then, after lining the plane up on what to me seemed a very small landing strip, touched down with the lightest of bumps. He taxied around, heading for a cluster of similar sized aeroplanes to ours and a group of buildings with a few people milling about and one of the first faces I saw was Kevin's, with a beaming smile stretched across his face. Once the plane had stopped and the engine was turned off and the pilot indicated that it was safe to open the doors and disembark, Kevin came over and after greeting his wife Audrey, shook my hands and said hi to Vee who was still sat behind me. Vee herself then got out and helped with the luggage, shopping and wheelchair that had all been carefully stowed away in the small luggage compartment at the rear. I could hear discussions taking place about how best to get me out, and it was unanimously agreed, that the simplest way, was the same way I got in.

Kevin then positioned me so that my bottom was close to the door and after again grabbing hold of my trouser waistband, inched me backwards. First onto the sill of the door and then onto the wing and then gradually down the wing to my waiting reassembled wheelchair, where extra pairs of strong hands were ready to lift me the final bit onto the cushion of my chair. I was very much relieved to be sitting comfortably and after a quick group photograph, one of many photo's that would be taken by Audrey over the remainder of my holiday, I asked Vee to tidy me up and once again check that my 'Conveen' was still intact. Again amazingly, after all the pulling about it was. Kevin then pushed me to a waiting golf buggy, transferred me into the front seat, loaded my chair, still intact, into the back along with our baggage and after taking hold of my shoulders with his right arm to support me, drove the buggy the short distance to the seashore and the awaiting boat that would take us the last leg of the journey to Soldier Cay. Loading me into the boat, once back in my chair, was not a problem. I was simply tipped back in my chair and then Kevin, who was standing inside the flat-bottomed skiff, pulled me up and over the side, whilst Audrey, who was holding onto my footrest, pushed. I was put near the rear where the steering wheel was and after the luggage and shopping was safely put aboard, the four of us set off to Soldier Cay. It was around 3.30 pm and still very hot and Kevin joked that as soon as he was clear of the harbour, he would turn the air-con on? This puzzled me, however, once we were out of the small harbour and into the more open sea, Kevin adjusted the throttle of the motor and as the nose of the skiff raised slightly, to indicate our picking up of speed, so the air flow around us increased. This brought about the cooling, the air-con we needed, after being in the sun for the fifteen minutes or so since getting out of the plane.

Having been awed by the colours and sights I saw whilst flying too Staniel Cay, sitting in the skiff, literally only inches away from the water, was another thing altogether. I could see the ripples caused by the wave action in the white sand, that's how clear the water was and once again the colours were spectacular. I allowed my right hand to hang over the side, so that the water, churned up as the boat sped along splashed it. The front edge of the baseball cap I had been given to protect me from the sun, was flapping about in the wind, meaning I had to pull it firmly down and for the thirty minutes or so it took to get to Soldier Cay, I just sat in silence, lost in wonderment at the sights that were unfolding in front of me as we journeyed on. Feeling the heat on my face as well as the cooling breeze, this really was my dream come true.

We passed a few of the other islands in the Exuma chain, some with buildings and signs of habitation on them, but most were just barren rocky outcrops with just a few seabirds perched on them. Then Kevin began to slow down and told us that Soldier Cay would soon be coming into view. As we got closer and I saw some of the familiar sights of the island, thanks to the photographs that had been emailed to me, the first thing that struck me, was the noise. If you have ever sat near a cricket in your garden or at the park, then you would have heard the noise it made as it signalled to others around it. Well, multiply that noise by tens of thousands and you would get somewhere near to what I was beginning to hear as the skiff drew closer and closer to the small marina we were heading for. I asked Kevin what was making the din and Kevin at first was surprised by the question, saying that, as people often say who live near airports or railway lines and busy roads, that they were so used to the noise around them, that they no longer noticed it. How on earth they could get used to such a racket and we were still thirty or forty yards offshore, was a surprise to me and it would be a noise I would notice, on and off, right up to our leaving. Anyway, he told me that the clamour came from the Cicada beetles that were all over the island and a few days later, I would be shown the evidence of their existence, through the discarded skins they shed as part of their apparently short life cycle. The other wildlife inhabiting the island were lots of other bugs, a few rodents, of which thankfully I would never see, a few small lizards, a small variety of birds and Kevin and Audrey's two dogs, Tassle and Gizmo, who, having heard the engine noise of the skiff, were standing by the berth awaiting our arrival with tails wagging.

Once off the skiff, I was transferred onto another golf buggy, the preferred method of getting about in the terrain that makes up these islands and driven over a very bumpy track to where I would be staying, the Beach House. On the way, Audrey stopped off at their home in order to quickly take indoors the shopping, some of which was ice cream, depositing the fragile goods in their fridge freezer out of the heat, which even at this hour of the afternoon was still quite hot. The Beach House was at the southern most part of the island, literally just a few yards away from the waves. A bungalow, square and of wooden construction standing some three or four feet off the ground with a few steps at the front leading to a veranda with a fine mesh screen surrounding it to keep the bugs out. The veranda led, via some double glazed double doors into the bungalow, which comprised of a small kitchen on your right, a living room ahead, two bedrooms ahead and to the left and the bathroom on the right. It was simple, clean and comfortable and mine for the next ten days.

After we had all set too in unpacking my things, quickly putting them away, Kevin asked if anything else needed doing. Having checked out how the main bedroom, the one with air conditioning in was organised, I asked that some of the furniture be taken out as I would not be using it and it would simply be in my way. Then I asked that the bed be repositioned, so that transferring into and out of it would be easier. This done, Kevin took Vee to her home, which was situated at the other end of the island; the first one we had passed after getting off the skiff. It was known as the staff quarters for obvious reasons. However, Vee didn't care what name it was known by, it was hers alone as the Beach House was for me. Apart from the four of us, the dogs and all the other wildlife, there was no one with us and no one else near us for several miles, so she relished the idea of having the house all to herself, where she could retreat for some personal space and quiet of her own.

Their departure meant I had for the first time, my own personal space. Up till this moment, there had always been someone near bye. I had a wander around my new home, made easy by the stone tile flooring and checked out where I could get too within the bungalow. The only area I could not access easily was the second bedroom and that was because that was where the spare furniture from my room had been stacked, so that was no loss to me. I ended my tour facing out of the double doors towards the sea and marvelled again at the view. There were a few trees near bye, a couple of palm trees and one or two varieties unknown to me. A lounger on the beach near the steps on my left and a hammock strung between two trees right on the waters edge, which as I've said, was only a few yards away from the house. The tide was out and a few rocks near the shoreline were being washed over by the shallow waves that were making their way in. There was the shrilling of the birds and when they went quiet, the beetles started up with their noise. The noise though was beginning not to bother me in the slightest, for regardless of the sound, it was so peaceful, if that makes any sense and I felt happy just being there. I had told Kevin and Audrey that I was so looking forward to being quiet and on my own and they, for the most part, took me to my word. Kevin had left me with some cold water and a glass of red wine, both of which were drunk and enjoyed in this quiet time on my own.

About an hour and a half later, somewhere around 6.00 pm, I heard the sound of a buggy coming down the track and a second later Kevin and Vee came into view. Between them they took me down the steps and loaded me into the buggy at the front and my chair in the back. Kevin then drove the short distance, about two hundred yards to their home and within a few seconds we were all sat in their kitchen having a cold drink and chatting ahead of dinner that Audrey was finishing off. Kevin had obviously been apprised of the problem of the brake on my chair coming off, because he had some tools ready. One of his main jobs on the island is the upkeep and maintenance of all the property and equipment, so it was no huge task for him to quickly reattach my brake. Once done, I felt whole again and secure in the knowledge that my transfers would be safe, thanks to my having two functioning brakes.

More wine for me followed that and after a lovely meal comprising of fish, we headed off to their lounge and chatted more about what had happened to make all of this possible. I don't remember what time it was, but I suddenly felt tired and after thanking Audrey for the meal, was taken down the by now dark track to my home. Through the glare of the lights from the golf buggy, I could see the myriad of bugs flying about. We had been warned of the high possibility of being bitten and the morning would prove that to be a reality, evidenced by the red welts on both Vee and myself. Vee got me settled quite quickly, she had easily picked up my routine and was having no trouble in getting me sorted in quick time on yet, as in Atlantis, another high bed and then, after turning off the air conditioning in my bedroom, but leaving the ceiling fan on, she left to be taken to her home by Kevin.

Day 5.

We had agreed the night before, that Vee would come to get me up at eight as was usual for me. I had at first toyed with the idea of getting up earlier, giving me more time to do more things. However, I decided that my enjoyment of the day's end, the evening meal and chat about the day or whatever, would be spoilt if I became too tired due to being up too early, so on this Monday morning, my first full day here on Soldier Cay, eight it was.

Getting dressed was simple and quick, a pair of shorts and sandals. A wash and a brush of my teeth in the bathroom, a shave and then over to the kitchen area where Kevin had brought over from their home, a pump action thermos to be used for my morning constitutional, my hot water breakfast. Vee by this time had tidied up my bedroom, sorted out my night drainage bag and was now boiling the kettle to fill the thermos with. As I was waiting, I asked Vee to help me over the small lip that formed part of the double doors separating the living room and the veranda, I had noticed a thermometer hanging just inside the outer door of the veranda and I was curious to see what it was reading. It was showing thirty degrees Celsius and this at only 9.00 am, what was the rest of the day going to be like I wondered?

As there was a table and chairs in the veranda, I decided to stay there for my water and when it was ready, Vee set it all out so that I could reach everything I would need. The thermos and my own cup from home, my book, which was a thriller I had borrowed from Kevin's collection and the walkie talkie to communicate with Kevin or Audrey should I need to. Kevin then appeared, having given us the hour or so we said it would take to get sorted and after checking that all was ok, he drove Vee off to their place so that she could join them for breakfast. Again I was on my own and with a cup of hot water on my lap tray, I looked out and once more revelled in the view, the heat and the sensation of being where I was.

At around 10.30 am I could hear again the sound of a golf buggy coming down the track, only there was two of them. Vee had obviously been given a lesson on how to drive one, as she was the first to appear followed closely by Kevin. They parked up and joined me on the veranda. The plan, Kevin said, was to have a tour of the island, to familiarise ourselves with it's simple layout and then to join Audrey in their home for lunch. So grabbing a hat and the camera I had borrowed from Charlotte Wheeler, the elder daughter of my mate Bob, I was loaded into the buggy Kevin had driven, leaving Vee's behind ready for our return, thus saving Kevin from constantly having to ferry Vee back and forth and off we went. As I have previously mentioned, the island is only approximately four acres in size, something like four hundred yards in length, so it didn't take too long to reach the far northern point where a gazebo had recently been built there. Having seen it, I was determined to spend some time in it, enjoying the obvious attractions of its different views and breeze that seemed more in evidence at this end of the island. We then passed by the marina we had arrived at yesterday and were told a little about the various boats that were moored there, then on past the staff quarters, Vee's bungalow and an area where the mail boat arrives to drop off their deliveries. From there we drove across to the east of the island and Kevin informed us that if we kept going east we would eventually reach Africa. This side of the island was rougher, unkempt, not used, other than for burning rubbish and dumping worn out items, old freezers etc. It was also more wind swept, more exposed to the open sea and it was evident by how choppy the water was, with white topped waves rolling in with a lot more force than the sheltered west side, the side where all the accommodation was situated.

In all there were six bungalows. The two Vee and myself were staying in, Kevin and Audrey's, called the Managers House. The Main House only used when the owner of the island, a Sandy Mactaggart stays. A bungalow called the Runaway, which the owner's wife, Cecile uses when she needs to get away for a while to write and to be by her self. Then finally a bungalow known as High View, because it's built on the highest point of the island with commanding views over that side of the island and indeed all other things to the west. Having seen the homes from the outside, Kevin promised that over the course of my stay, he would show me around each one properly, giving me the full guided tour.

We ended up, as arranged, outside their home and were soon inside out of the midday heat. Audrey asked how things had been and also inquired if there was anyone at home who would appreciate a phone call. It would be 5.00 pm back home and for sure Ilona would be around, so as I called out my home number, Audrey dialled it for me and then passed over the phone once she heard the dialling tone. Ilona answered on the fourth ring and though it took her a little getting used too, she quickly picked up on the delay between speaking and receiving a response to what you have said. Once she mastered that, we had a nice chat, with a brief summary of how the five days had so far gone. It not being my phone bill, I didn't want too long a conversation and Ilona appreciated that and was grateful for my contacting her, if just to reassure her that all was well. I then asked if it would be ok to phone my mate Bob Wheeler up and it being ok, we did the same as before, with me calling out the number and Audrey dialling. Once again, I gave Bob a quick fill in as to my journey and time here so far. He was really pleased for me, knowing as he did the trouble I have had in the past and what it had taken to get here. Audrey was in the process of preparing lunch and asked what I would like. In the end, because of the heat, I was happy with a round of toast, much to the surprise of Audrey who seemed concerned, as I suppose any host would, that I wasn't eating enough. After reassurances from me that I really don't have that big an appetite, especially in the summer, she duly obliged and made my lunch for me.

After lunch I was taken back to the Beach House and I asked to be sat in the shade of the trees on the seashore where the hammock was strung. Kevin got a table for me and brought my hot water, though I preferred the bottle of cold water that he also brought. I had my camera with me still and so took several photographs of the scene in front of me. I tried to create a panoramic picture using three separate ones and when eventually the pictures were developed, they turned out ok considering my limited use of hands. I watched the gentle waves coming and going and noticed that the tide was slowly coming in. It really was a peaceful and restful place and I'm not going to apologise for saying that over and over again. I had thought that Worthing offered me rest when I went there for my respite breaks, but this place had that beat hands down.

At around 3.00 pm Kevin and Vee made their way back and I was taken to a small white sandy beach known as 'Tiki Beach'. I was going for a swim and whilst my paddle with the dolphins back in Nassau had been in salt water, this was the genuine article, the Caribbean Sea. The first thing I noticed at the beach, which was only about thirty yards long, was the chair that Kevin had made and had mentioned in one of the many emails sent to me. He had asked questions about the seat width of my wheelchair for the very purpose of getting his creation right and it was very similar to the chair I had used to swim with the dolphins. A white plastic patio chair bolted to a frame, with two large balloon tyres at the back, again to make crossing the soft sand easy. There was also a little hut at the top of the beach, called the 'Tiki hut' and a sun lounger next to it. Between Kevin and Vee, I was lifted from the buggy straight onto Kevin's creation and then wheeled over the sand to the waters edge. Audrey was already in the water holding onto a bunch of, what she called, 'noodles'! Why they were called noodles I never got to ask, but in describing them, I would simply say that they resembled lagging, or insulation, similar to that you might have around the pipes of your central heating boiler. They were about four feet in length, of various colours and were to be used as flotation aids. Once the chair became buoyant, due to the large tyres, I was lifted out and laid on my back in the water. Then, Audrey pushed one noodle under my back and one under my neck and that was it, I was on my own. I was floating in the warmest sea I had ever been in and with what must surely have been the biggest smile on my face thus far I was off. I began paddling away with my simple swimming stroke and feeling the biggest buzz I could ever imagine.

Only it wasn't, because after leaving me alone, but not too alone, for about half an hour, Kevin came up to me and asked if I had ever snorkelled and did I fancy a go!

I have said before, that me being in water is a real issue, I'm not a natural swimmer and certainly not now since the accident. It's a job and a half for me to stay afloat and swim, hence the need for the noodles to keep me from sinking. Turning over then and having my face under water was a thought way beyond my imagination. No I had never snorkelled, nor did I ever think I would get the opportunity, but Kevin was offering me the chance to have a go, so I had a go.

They had a couple of masks on the beach and after finding the right one for me and after being taught how to grip the gum shield in my mouth and to breath through it, Kevin slowly turned me over whilst Audrey made sure the noodle remained in place under my chest. As I felt the water closing in around my face, panic set in and whilst I had every confidence in Kevin, confidence in my own ability to breath whilst underwater was somewhat lacking. My brain was telling me that this was unnatural and I began to take short fast breaths. Kevin turned me back over and asked if I was ok, reassuring at the same time that all was well and telling me to try and relax and to slow my breathing. I nodded my head and was slowly turned again. This time I felt a little less panicky, but was still taking fast breaths, however, after only a few seconds I realised I wasn't drowning, that I was breathing air ok and so forced myself to slow down my breathing and relax. Suddenly I was aware of where I was, under water. The mask makes visibility under water extremely clear, not that the water wasn't already clear anyway and I began to look around and take in the scenery about me. To be honest, because of where we were situated, close to the shoreline of Tiki beach, there wasn't a great deal to see apart from Kevin's feet, the white sand and a few shells that were dotted around, so I began to move my head about to get a greater view. My view did improve and I could see further out and around me, but because I had moved my head so much, my breathing had a gurgling sound to it as seawater was getting into the snorkel. Kevin turned me over once more and explained to me what I was doing wrong and advised me as to the optimum position to have my face to get the better view, but also prevent the water getting into the snorkel. Turning back over for the third time, I realised that there was no sense of panic at all; my breathing remained unchanged as my face entered the water and I smiled inwardly at my new gained confidence in what I was doing and in what I had achieved. I felt Kevin moving and soon we were out into deeper water, ending up next to some wooden beams that made up part of a small jetty for mooring a boat. His purpose in moving became obvious straight away, there were several small fish swimming around the beams and I was presented with my first close encounter with fish in their natural habitat. A truly wonderful feeling and again I smiled inwardly as I thought that I was doing now more than I ever dreamt I would be and this was still only my first full day. After a few minutes, Kevin walked back to the shallows of the beach and after turning me over, took the mask and snorkel off me and asked how I was. My smile must have said it all because he smiled back and letting me go to have another swim, wandered off. As I swam, I turned my head to orientate myself to the beach and noticed that Audrey was taking Vee through the basics of snorkelling and she too was enjoying, also for the first time, the experiences I had just gone through.

Sadly it was over so quickly and we were heading back to the Beach House to get ready for the evening. I had dried very quickly in the warm afternoon air, but my skin had that salty taste to it you get from swimming in the ocean, so the first thing I did was have a shower. The shower in the Beach House was actually outside the Beach House! A door on the outside of my bathroom opened out into small wooden cubicle with planking at the height of knee to shoulder. The rest was covered with the same fine mesh that was around the veranda, again there to keep the bugs out. This meant that for the most part you were outside as you showered, another first for me and truthfully not a very comfortable one, not because of being outdoors as such, I'm not a prude and in any case there are no near neighbours who might complain if anything was visible. No, it was uncomfortable because as soon as I became wet, the gentle breeze that blew around the shower cubicle, felt like a blizzard to me and because I was sheltered from the sun, I quickly became cold. Thankfully Vee soon had me washed and dried and it was only a matter of getting on the bed to get fully dried, dressed and then back into my chair after Vee first dried it. Not having my normal shower chair with me meant I had to use my manual chair, which was not a problem, or so I thought at the time! So, once in my sitting room with a cup of hot water in my hands, waiting to be collected for the evening meal, I soon warmed up and all was well again.

The evening with Vee, Kevin and Audrey was once again a lovely time, sharing in some friendly banter about the day and about my many new achievements. This along with a fine meal with a glass or two of wine or beer, depending on your preference, made for the perfect end to my first full day on Soldier Cay.

Day 6.

Kevin put in an early appearance soon after I was up and about on this Tuesday morning; Vee's arrival at their home for breakfast would have been the obvious signal that I was up. He came armed with some cables, which once connected to a laptop computer, enabled my recently bought 'Ipod' to be charged, giving me music to listen to whilst on my own waiting for the day to unfold. I had been advised to bring along a selection of music for this very purpose and instead of lugging about my old portable CD player, and a dozen or so CD's, I was told by Vee to get with it and buy myself the modern gadget for listening to music.

I'm not a techno wizard and it's not my natural inclination to dash out to the shops to buy the latest must have gadget, but whilst my carry anywhere, jog-proof CD player is ok when I go to Worthing for my breaks, I realised that all that extra weight and bulk would be silly to carry such a distance and so to the shops I went to buy myself one. Then Temujin, my wife's oldest boy from her first marriage, helped me to download my favourite CD's onto my laptop and then into the 'Ipod' and I was away and very impressed I was too. It is so easy to use and extremely small and compact and made it ideal for taking away with me. Its incredible capacity enabled me to fill it with more music than I could have listened to, had I carried the loose CD's with me. So, after beavering away for a few minutes in the corner of the sitting room, where the base station for the 'Ipod' was plugged in, Kevin pressed a button and the room filled with a song from an all time favourite singer of mine, Eva Cassidy. I had first heard her music at a dinner party at Dieter and Penny's and have been a fan ever since and though I have an eclectic taste when it comes to music, very much a mood man, I think her voice is especially beautiful. Kevin then left me to my music, to my book and to catching up with writing an account of my time in the Bahamas, from which I am now writing this story in full.

I started to write the journal, more as a way of retelling the story to my wife. She always loves to hear in as much detail what I've been up to and as I'm usually a got there did this or that and then came home type of storyteller, I thought it prudent to write a few notes in a notepad, recording the amazing events of each day to help with my recounting of my adventures, and I'm glad I did. There would be no way I could ever do justice to my time in the Bahamas by simply going through it from memory. Each sentence in my pad was packed with hours of events and it has been simple so far to write it up in full.

The morning appeared to fly bye and I had not even noticed the time, so busy had I been with my writing and so engrossed was I with my book. I had not thought about wanting to be outside, even though it was yet another glorious day. It was only the coming noise of the golf buggy, signalling the arrival of Kevin and Vee that got me to raise my head and to realise how advanced the time was.

Lunch for me when we all met up later was a banana. This made the other three laugh as much as the toast had the previous day, but I was happy with that. I was also very thirsty, having drunk very little water due to my far away state of mind, a happy and contented one so I topped myself up with several large beakers of cold juice. After lunch, around 2.00 pm, we went down to the marina and after getting into the skiff, we went for a trip around Soldier Cay. We then did a tour around the neighbouring islands, one of which was owned by an actor by the name of Johnny Depp and the other the Agar Khan. Illustrious company indeed, even if no one was at home for the duration of my stay. Once again it was the beautiful seas and scenery that captivated me, and the warmth of the day after being indoors for what felt like the most part of it.

As we drew nearer to Soldier Cay, it was announced, that as it was thought we might go snorkelling out in deeper water later in the week, it would be a good idea to practice getting me out of the boat and into the water. This was done by Kevin first anchoring the boat in about five foot of water, just off Tiki Beach. Audrey then climbed out and stood at the side of the boat, whilst Kevin and Vee between them, lifted me out of the wheelchair and perched me on the edge of the boat, with my feet just dangling in the water. Kevin then gently lowered me down, so that eventually my legs were beginning to float and Audrey, having positioned herself to take my weight, controlled my entry into the water, ensuring that I was safely on my back. The whole process went really well, the two of them, previous to actually doing it, had obviously thought it through and in only a few seconds the floats were under my back and I was on my own swimming about. As the 'Meerkat' would say, "Simples"!

Once the swimming session was over and I was back at my house, I decided to sit by the hammock again, enjoying the outdoor air, much cooler now, as it was around 6pm. I drank some water and watched the waves creeping up the beach noticing, once again, that the tide was slowly coming in.

Kevin first appeared around the corner this time, closely followed by Vee, who, once I was inside got me dressed for another pleasant evening at Kevin and Audrey's for another vegetarian meal. Now don't get me wrong, I'm more than happy with a salad bowl, or pasta dish, or the fresh taste of newly caught fish, especially after a hot day and a busy one as this had been, but at the back of my mind was the craving for some red meat. Vee is a vegetarian and to include her in the evenings and to prevent Audrey from having to prepare a separate meal for her, we were all happy, for the moment, to eat the delicious meals she cooked up for us, but more on that later.

Day 7.

I quickly realised, once I was alone for my hot water breakfast, that I was feeling quite tired after all the swimming I did yesterday, a rather pleasant feeling for me, as I had long forgotten what it felt like to be tired from physical exertion. I was also very tender around my chest. This was due to my lying on my back in the sea as I swam about, getting myself at the same time, a little sunburnt. My normal sitting position when I sunbathe at home means that my chest and tummy very rarely gets in the full sun. In fact after sunbathing at home, when I lie flat on my back in bed, I look like, according to Annie Holdsworth, a dear friend from Worthing who helped me on a more recent holiday, a 'Neapolitan Ice Cream', with layers of red then white appearing from my chest down to my tummy. So lying on my back whilst swimming yesterday, meant that my whole front had been exposed to the glare of the sun and as a result I felt a little tender. I decided therefore to stay out of the full sun as much as possible today, giving myself a chance to recuperate a little from my tiredness and giving my skin a chance to calm down. After all, it was only Wednesday and there were plenty more opportunities ahead to enjoy the beautiful hot weather. So when Kevin appeared, as he did every morning for a chat, I told him I would like to go to the gazebo at the Northern tip of the island.

The gazebo, as mentioned earlier, was fairly new, having been built by Audrey's brother Pete, when he recently visited the island. It was well placed, having great views and a stronger cooling breeze, as it was more exposed than the other parts of the island I had sat at so far. I was left with plenty of water, my writing pad and pen, the walkie-talkie, a book and reassurances that someone would pop by every now and then to check on me. Once the buzz of the golf buggy had gone and I felt again all-alone, I pushed myself around the gazebo, enjoying the new views and as always the beautiful scenery that made this place so special. I had a drink, sat at an angle that afforded me a good view of the ocean and kept me out of the breeze enough to stop the pages of my journal from flapping about and began to write. I had been writing for a few minutes and to relieve the ache that was just starting in my neck and shoulders, brought on by the position I sit in to read or write, I sat up straight and began to twist my head from side to side and as I did so, something moving in the corner of my peripheral vision caught my attention. I turned the chair slowly to get a better view and was greeted by the sight of a humming bird not six feet away feeding from the plants growing nearby. The bird continued feeding for about thirty seconds, flying from plant to plant and then flew away; another wow moment.

Kevin reappeared around midday and back at their home, lunch for me was a bowl of fruit salad and one of Audrey's home made and still warm banana nut muffin and very tasty it was too.

Still determined to stay out of the sun for the afternoon, I was taken to the Marina Beach and told that the plans for the rest of the day had been changed somewhat and could I guess what might be about to happen! Well as I pondered on that, a couple of things came to mind. We were all sat under the shade of the trees on the top edge of the beach facing out to the sea. Kevin and Audrey knew I had opted to stay out of the water today, so it had to be either something on the water, a boat trip of some kind, or something over the water, a plane, maybe a seaplane! Suddenly the radio that Kevin was holding squawked into action and Kevin made some response and at that moment I guessed it had to be a seaplane. A few seconds after having had that thought, a seaplane came roaring into view. It came in low over the sea, curling around the island across from where we were sitting. It then came straight towards our position and climbed flying directly overhead. After it flew around for a few more seconds, it then landed and approached our beach.

The pilot was obviously a good friend of Kevin and Audrey's and after they had all said hi to each other and caught up briefly with news of life on the island and work, Vee and I were introduced to him. A discussion then took place as to how to get me into the plane and soon I found myself being lifted out of my chair, carried through the shallow water to where the plane was waiting and being posted through the tiny door and into an even tinier seat at the rear.

So small was the seat in fact, that my eventual sitting position was incredibly uncomfortable. In order to actually stay where I was placed, my bottom had to go right back into where the backrest joins the seat. Normally, in order to sit upright in any other chair, my bottom is away from the backrest, helping me to lean back slightly, gaining my balance and so staying upright. This wasn't possible in this situation and as a result I was forced to lean forward and could only stay in a position where I could look out, by holding onto a strut to the right of the front passenger seat, where Vee now was and push myself into as upright a position as I could. All of which took quite a lot of effort. The pilot asked for confirmation that we were both ok and I simply smiled, there was not a lot else I could do in that situation. He then taxied into position ready for take off. The sea was flat calm and as we speeded up I was glad it was, as the bumps, even on this calm sea, went right through my body and my arm, which by this time was already beginning to ache. The flight was a short one thankfully; taking in pretty much the same views we had had from the skiff, when Kevin took us on a tour of the nearby islands the other day, the only difference being the height and speed we were travelling at. I was glad it was a short trip in the end, even though the whole thing was a great treat, with again spectacular views, but by the time we were preparing to land I was getting dizzy. This was being brought on by the strain on my right arm and the position I had put my body in to look out the window. Once down and by the beach from where we had started, I could relax my posture and boy oh boy was I happy to get lifted out and put back into my chair. I doubt though that the pilot was! Apparently he is quite fussy about his plane, keeping it as spotlessly clean as he can. Well, because of my contorted sitting position, my 'Conveen' had become separated and in all probability there would be a damp patch on the rear seat. I never heard any comeback, so maybe it went un-noticed or in the end was no big deal for him.

A short while later, after thanking the pilot and having a fresh 'Conveen' put on, I was once more sat by the hammock near my house, with water and my book and I was all set for a couple of hours of peace and quiet. However, within thirty minutes or so I heard a noise in the distance and saw a motorboat coming into view. I was suddenly struck by how much of a strange sensation it was, seeing something and someone other than the four of us on the island. I had met with the pilot of the seaplane yes, but he was expected and for that short while, part of the group. This felt like an intrusion into my private space and even though it was several hundred yards away, it annoyed me it being there. Things were about to get worse though.

The boat settled in one position and I got back to reading my book, keeping up with my fluid intake and generally enjoying where I was. When suddenly, an awful piercing noise reached my ears and shattered the quiet. I looked up again in the direction of the recent arrival and saw two jet-skis doing small circles around the boat. They then set off in a much larger looping turn and were pretty soon fairly close to where I was sitting. Now I felt angry and the daftest thought came into my head. How dare they, I thought, come so close when there was so much empty space to play in, in every direction you looked? They buzzed about for twenty minutes or so and then headed off, leaving me with a strange sensation. One of not being on my own after all, one that told me that the real world outside of the island, still did exist in the form of one boat and two jet-skis!

After being dressed for the evening and arriving at Kevin and Audrey's home, I was alerted to the fact that my wife Ilona, had rang and left a message. Kevin dialled my home number for me and we had a chat for a few minutes. No alarm or panic in her calling, she just wanted to chat. Dinner that evening was a pasta and mushroom salad dish and after talking through the day's events, I was in bed by 10.30 pm and found myself reflecting on the fact that that was the end of the first week. I was amazed with that thought, that I had done so much in such a short space of time and yet it had felt so much longer than a week. I always say that a proper holiday feels longer than the time you have away and this was a proper holiday.

Day 8.

Thursday started in the usual way and I had just started my hot water breakfast and writing up my journal when the clouds suddenly got dark and it began to rain! It was so unexpected and out of the blue; if you pardon the pun that I put my pad and pen down and watched the rain falling. It only lasted ten minutes and hardly made a difference to the parched ground outside. The temperature had dropped slightly during the time it rained, but once the heavy clouds shifted away it soon picked up again, much to my relief because after staying out of the sun pretty much all day yesterday, I was looking forward to being out and sunbathing once more.

When Kevin arrived for his morning chat and brief about the day, I commented on the rain and he said that it had been the second squall of the day. Apparently and unknown to me, it had first rained at around 5.30 that morning. I was obviously fast asleep at the time and with the ceiling fan on and my earplug in had slept right through it. Once the chat about the rain was over, we got talking about the plans for this day, which Kevin said involved a boat trip out into deeper water to feed the sharks! My expression must have been the one he was expecting and with a smile, he went on to explain that there is a well-known area out in the ocean nearby, where divers go down to the reef to swim with the sharks. Harmless reef sharks, if there is such a thing as a harmless shark, gather there and we were going out with some food to feed them. He reassured me that there were no plans to get in the water with them, unless that is I wanted too! I, without hesitation, said no. As Kevin left, saying that he would be back around 10.00, I reflected on those individuals who brave getting into the ocean to purposely interact with sharks. It would be akin, I thought, to a steak dropping onto my plate from nowhere and begging to be eaten. Definitely not for me and I'm pretty sure that if I left them alone today and left them to their own environment, then they should me.

There wasn't a great deal of time left before Kevin was due back, so rather than carry on with my journal, I got my things together ready for the trip. As I picked up my borrowed camera, I decided to take some photos of my house, views looking in from the patio and views out. I'm not great with cameras, my lack of dexterity in my fingers means I'm a little clumsy, but I took a few anyway. I suppose the whole point of a digital camera, apart from the quality of the photographs, is that you can simply edit out any that don't turn out quite right and keep the ones you like. In the end the finished product wasn't at all bad, if I do say so myself.

By 10.30 I was on the skiff with Vee and with a wave from Audrey, who was staying behind for this trip, we set off. It had indeed warmed up after the much cooler start to the day than normal and once again I was thankful for that little bit of sea breeze aided by the forward momentum of the skiff. Twenty minutes into our journey, something moving forty yards or so to my right caught my eye. I tracked the movement and realised that it was a dolphin, heading pretty much in the same direction as us. I got Kevin's attention and pointed across and as he slowed down he said that he thought it was a turtle. I told him I thought it was a dolphin and right on cue it came up for air, confirming my belief as right. Kevin then tried steering the skiff a little closer, without wanting to alarm it and by matching it's speed, which wasn't very quick, we followed the dolphin for several minutes, until we had to change course and head away from it. Now, having swam with dolphins only a few days previously, you might be surprised to hear that I found the experience of being near this wild animal, out in it's natural habitat, doing it's own thing, more exciting than stroking the captive and very tame dolphins I had been with. I imagine those who have been on safari and witnessed the wild animals of Africa out in their huge game parks, where the life of the animals is a more natural one, as apposed to viewing them in the zoos, would possibly say the same.

At around 11.00 we arrived at the island that was the home and office of the park warden. It had pleased me to hear from Kevin earlier, that in order to protect the natural beauty and wildlife of the area, a huge chunk of the Exuma Chain of islands had been turned into a park, protected by law and the wardens that regularly patrolled the vast area looking out for illegal fishing and those intent on doing damage to the coral.

Kevin steered the skiff into the bay of the island and as we approached the beach he pointed to what appeared to be a skeleton. As we got closer we saw that it was indeed a skeleton, a skeleton of a whale that had apparently died on the beach and had been left there, turning eventually into a bit of a tourist attraction.

We dutifully took photographs of it and then headed out of the bay, out into deeper water. This was easily denoted by the fact that the water was both darker and much choppier. Away from the protection of the islands and the shallowness of the sea around the islands, the open sea reverted back to it's normal state, with waves which rocked the flat bottomed skiff and caused me to take a firmer grip of my chair. Kevin, who was following a nautical version of a sat-nav, asked us to look out for a white buoy, which should be nearby, saying that was where we were heading for. I was sitting down and with the height the waves were reaching, had a very poor view ahead and as Kevin was standing up, it was he who saw the buoy first and steered us towards it. The skiff was rocking quite badly, so it was a job for him to tie the boat up to the buoy, but once he had done so and the skiff had turned with the wind and the waves, the rocking eased somewhat and it became bearable and I felt safe.

After a refreshing drink of water for ourselves, Kevin got out a large plastic container filled with scraps of meat, which Audrey had prepared, with which we were going to feed the sharks. Vee and I were looking around, with a little bit of dread, at the possibility of coming face to face with sharks, but we couldn't see any. Kevin told us to be patient and sure enough, a minute later, these dark and ominous shapes began to appear circling around the skiff, just below the water. I began to throw the sliced meat as far as I could away from me, which with my grip was not that far, only three or four feet. As soon as the food had hit the water, other smaller fish dashed from nowhere and grabbed it and swam away, leaving the sharks trailing in their wake. Of all the meat I took out of this large container, I could not say for certain, how much of it the sharks themselves actually got to eat. But in the end that wasn't the point. Being only a few feet away from a dozen or so 10 to 12 feet long reef sharks was and although the trip back to Soldier Cay was a more bumpy but fun ride because we were into the wind, it was yet another one of those wow moments and was to become a lasting memory, with again some great photo's.

We got back at 1.00 pm, the hottest part of the day and headed straight for the cool and comfort of Kevin and Audrey's home. I had a tuna sandwich for lunch, a little ironic after our time with the sharks and because it was such a hot day, decided to wait where I was until it cooled a little. Whilst we waited, I asked if would be ok to phone my mother. She had asked that if it were possible, to phone her to let her now how things were and as I had already called my wife and then best friend, I thought I ought to. She was both surprised and delighted to hear my voice and after a quick chat with her and my younger sister, Jean, who was with her, said my goodbyes and hung up. Audrey then asked if I would like a game of 'Scrabble', to which I agreed. I'm usually quite good with words, but I met a better player on this occasion and for every other game we played during the remainder of my stay. Now, even though my average score of nearing two hundred points over all the games we played was an ok score for me, it was short of what Audrey was achieving. I have always been a competitive individual, in any sport or game and whilst losing stung, I regarded it as good fun and an active way of passing the time away.

At 3.30 pm the sting had gone out of the sun and we all headed to the 'Tiki' beach for another wonderful swim and another go at snorkelling. I felt a lot more at ease this time when I was turned face down and enjoyed more of the experience. Kevin then said that because of what was hopefully going to happen in the next few days, he needed to fetch the motorboat so that we could practice getting into it from the sea. So, whilst I lay on my back and swam a little more, he went off to get the boat. As I lay there swimming or just floating, I pondered on what Kevin had meant when he said, what might be happening in the next few days. But to be truthful, I just didn't care or give it too much thought, because to my way of thinking and at that precise moment, nothing could better what I was presently doing, or had done over the past week. How wrong I was to be!

I heard, more than saw Kevin arriving and once the boat was safely anchored, I was floated over to the rear, or stern I suppose, of the motorboat, the 'Carina'. Across the stern of the 'Carina', at just about sea level, was a grill that protruded out about 18 inches which was used for putting items on from the sea. So for example, if someone was in the water, it was ideally placed for him or her, to put any heavy or bulky equipment on before getting in the boat. They could then retrieve their things from a position of security, from within the boat, rather than attempting to put things all the way into the boat from the sea. This grill was what they were going to use to get me into the boat. Both Kevin and Audrey lifted me with my back to the stern until I was sat on the grill. Then, whilst Audrey held me and stopped me from falling over, Kevin climbed into the boat, grabbed hold of me under my shoulders and pulled me up onto the padded area that covered a small section at the stern. Once I felt my bottom on the padded area, I lay down flat leaving my lower legs dangling over the stern. Then, once Audrey and Vee were aboard, between the three of them, they positioned me into my wheelchair that Kevin had already loaded in when he went to fetch the boat. It may sound complicated, but in fact it was a simple enough manoeuvre, thanks in the main to the physical strength of both Kevin and Audrey and the thinking that had gone into the process. With a grin of satisfaction that said a plan had come together and worked, Kevin said that that was how I would be getting out from the sea from now on. Getting into the sea from the boat we had already practiced, so the whole routine was ready to put into good use.

Back on dry land a few minutes later, gave me a final opportunity, for this day, to do some more sunbathing and even though it was around 5.00 pm, it was still hot enough, so that twenty minutes was plenty for me. Once satisfied, it was back to my house for a cooling shower. I was then dressed for the evening and with a glass of wine to hand; I waited to be collected, noticing once again that my shoulders were stinging from the sun. Oh what joyful pain!

Dinner that evening was another first for me; lobster. I have never eaten so many different varieties of fish in my whole life as I have so far on this holiday and tonight's meal was yet another treat. Once the table was cleared, Kevin invited me to a few games of backgammon, which I was glad to do and of the three games we played I won two. They were all very close finishes and when we played again later in the week the result was reversed, so a fair outcome in the end. By 9.45 pm the full and busy day was getting to me, so I excused myself and was taken home. On the way down the track, I looked up into the night sky, something all of us must have done at some point in our life and marvelled at the sight that met my eyes. I have, of course, looked up more than once since being on the island, but tonight there was a clarity about the sky that was new, new and awesome. At home when looking up, my view had always been spoilt by the light pollution, caused by the streetlights or the town and city lights that get reflected back up and so spoiling what should be seen. One of the things I had been made aware of before coming over, was the fact that, as the island is so isolated, they are in total darkness and being curious about the night sky, as I'm sure we all are, I intended to spend some time during one of the nights, looking up into what I hoped would be a totally different view to the one I was so used too. Well I was not disappointed on this occasion, the sky was so full of stars and it was an unbelievable sight. Even with the naked eye, I could see more than I ever had and once in my house, I asked Kevin if I could lie on the floor somewhere one night to have a good look. He said he would arrange it, saying it had been something he had done himself many times.

Day 9.

Once up and about, the most obvious thing about this new day was how much stronger the breeze was, it was most certainly going to impact upon whatever activities Kevin had planned for me, so it was a case of waiting until he arrived to find out.

It was around 9.30 when I heard Kevin's golf buggy coming down the track and looking out from the veranda, I was pleased to see Audrey was with him. She had come along she said, to check if everything was all right with the house still, had I any laundry, bed sheets or clothes that wanted washing. Whilst she popped off to check the wash basket, Kevin told me that both Audrey and him had a lot of little odd jobs to catch up on and so whilst they cracked on with them, I was going to put on the veranda at the 'Main House', the owner's house for the morning. That was ok with me I said, as I knew it would be out of the early morning breeze, but in the sun, with options for me to sit in the shade should

I wish. Audrey put down the little bag she had brought with her in case there was any washing and produced from her pocket a nail clipping set. I had mentioned the previous night that my nails were getting long and she had promised to trim them for me, which she did. Whilst she was doing my nails, I mentioned how the pockets on my trousers and swimming shorts had torn. Kevin had caused this, as he used the sides of my trousers and shorts, as a grip, to lift me up from behind when getting me in and out of my chair. Vee would hold me under my knees and lifted at the same time as Kevin. A manoeuvre that worked fine, except that if his grip was not in the right place, then my pockets would take the brunt of my weight and tear. She said she would look at them and before too long I found myself on the veranda of the 'Main House'.

I quickly discovered why it was chosen as the 'Main House', the view of the sea and the neighbouring islands was particularly lovely. The veranda was a large one, with tables and chairs for outside dining and plenty of space for me to wander around and shade should I need it. Audrey placed a bowl of sugar on the table I was sitting at, at the furthest corner away from me. I had seen her do this fairly often and knew and looked forward to what was coming. The sugar was to attract the local birds, known as 'Banana Quits', who seemed to be all over the island and doing very well, maybe because of Audrey's generous and constant supply of sugar. As soon as I had had a drink and then began to catch up with my journal, they started to arrive, in no way fazed by my presence. I can describe them best, as a small delicate bird with a yellow chest, a white throat and white stripes down the back of their heads. They have a small curved beak, which they use to reach the nectar from the plants, hence the sweet tooth and in flight their tails fan out.

They were a delight to watch and kept me well entertained during the two hours I had to myself, to do my reading and writing. In those two hours, as well as bringing my journal up to date, I had written a letter of thanks to the owner of the Island, Sandy, which I intended to send by email upon my return home.

At 11.30, Kevin arrived and took me on a quick tour of the house proper. I, as many, I'm sure, have never been in a millionaire's home and I was not really sure of what to expect. What greeted my eyes though, was not a typical glossy magazine' representation of a millionaire's home. It was simple, comfortable and not too ornate in any sense. Kevin said it was just as Sandy liked it, he was not a flashy showy man and it was reflected in how he preferred his holiday home.

From there it was back to Kevin's home for lunch, which for me today, because of the heat, was just a yogurt. More games of backgammon in the early afternoon with Kevin which he won 2 – 1 and then scrabble with Audrey, which she won again. This took us nicely to around 3 pm and the time of day cool enough to be out and about. We all went down to the marina and got aboard the motorboat and from there went just a short distance away from the island, to a small group of rocks known as the 'Aquarium'. Once secured to a buoy, I was helped into a flotation jacket and then Kevin reminded me of the plan of action for getting me from my chair and into the sea. Well it worked well enough, as it had at the 'Tiki" beach rehearsal. In fact it was a little better, because Kevin was able to use his grip on the flotation jacket I was now wearing and not my shoulders to lower me and although I had a few anxious moments, I soon had things other than the drop into the sea to think about. For one the water, being a lot deeper, was also a lot colder than the shallows I had previously been swimming in and I'm not great in cold water. The second concern for me was how choppy the water was and I was regularly having waves splashing over my face, again something I had not yet experienced until now.

Kevin quickly appeared alongside me and after adjusting the jacket slightly, so that I floated level and fitting the snorkel and mask over my head, prepared me for the turn onto my stomach. Once over, I was a bit panicky for a few seconds, but soon got into the swing of things and with my breathing calm and regular, I felt Kevin begin to guide me over to the rocks and to where the fish were congregated.

The rocks were known as the 'Aquarium' for the obvious reason that there were lots of fish in the area and once acclimatised to where I was, I began to pick them out. Audrey was doing her best to help out I found out later, because she was throwing bread near to where we were swimming to attract them to us and to us they came. They were literally within touching distance and although I was too slow to actually touch them, it was nevertheless fun trying. The water in that area, Kevin had told me prior to getting in, was about twenty feet deep, however, it was still crystal clear and I could easily see the seabed and the views all around me were fabulous. The colours and variety of the fish was a sight to behold. As were the different coral and rock formations, all were extraordinary and pretty soon the coldness of my environment and the splashing over my head were forgotten as I marvelled at what I saw about me. Another thing that amazed me about that swim and it only came to light later in the evening, when Audrey took me through the daily photograph update, was the fact that for some of the time I was on my own! I had felt Kevin's presence and firm grip on my jacket for most of the time, but, unbeknown to me, Kevin had at one point let go and the photographs of me face down, snorkelling on my own, came as a pleasurable shock and surprise.

Having practised getting back into the boat the other day, it was no great hardship to do so now. Truth be told, it was even easier because Kevin, as with getting me in, could use the jacket to grip me, rather than my wet and slippery body and soon I was being wrapped in towels to get dry and warm. I again had a smile on my face that must have said it all. It was then Vee's turn to have a go and after a few minutes of reassurance from Audrey, she was quite happily swimming about on her own. I asked Kevin, had I been brought back out of the water so soon after going in, because it was colder than I was used too? He had a quizzical expression on his face and then informed me, that I had been in for at least forty-five minutes, which came as a complete surprise to me. It had passed so quickly, adding meaning to the old cliché, that time passes quickly when your having fun. Well I was and it saddened me a little when, after Vee had had her swim, we had to leave and headed back to Kevin and Audrey's for a drink and a piece of cake.

As I sat in my house around 6 pm that night, reflecting upon the day and the holiday as a whole, I pondered on the fact that I have, at times, found it hard to put into words, the feelings and emotions that each new day and the adventures that filled them, into my journal. The yellow pad is on my lap, pen poised and I feel strangely empty of things to include, other than the few simple sentences that I write. These describe, pretty much in diary form, the basic events of the day. I started the journal as a fun thing, a way to help me recount the holiday to my wife. It's only much later in my office in Derby, as I fill out those sentences into paragraphs and pages, whilst watching every now and then the actual photographs taken by Audrey, or those taken on the camera I borrowed, as they scroll down on the special picture frame my older brother John bought me, that those feelings and emotions come readily back into focus. The week plus so far, has been a tremendous and eye opening experience for me, one that words can never do justice too. So I plod on with my journal come diary, telling about my snorkelling and the other many wonderful experiences. I'm simply happy in the knowledge, that there is at least something to share when I get back home, never thinking it would turn into an adventure itself, in writing it out in full as I am now many months later.

My journal up to date, a glass of wine drunk and there was even time to watch another short sharp rainstorm pass by, before I was once again loaded into the buggy and taken for our evening meal. It was another nice meal, a quiche and salad, with plenty of chitchat and thoughts for us all about the day. Had I been ok with the method of entry into the sea, had I recognised any of the fish I saw and would I like a book they had that showed some of the fish native to the islands. The evening soon passed and my yawning was the signal to head back to my place, to brush my teeth, go to the toilet and bed. This was the time of day that both Vee and myself hated. We called it the 'Mozzy Run'. By now the breeze had lessened, as it did most nights, allowing all the nighttime insects to do their worse, as they had done to us both from the start of our stay on the island and I had counted, before this night, at least fifteen bites on my body. Red welts that, where I could feel as normal, were itching like mad. Poor Vee had it far worse than me; she has fair skin, which seemed to attract them like metal filings to a magnet and because she had to come with me, to help me, then make her way back to her home at the other end of the island, spent more time being attacked and subsequently, had far more bites that were more visible than mine. She must have been in agony, but if she was, I don't remember her saying too much about it, much to her credit.

Day 10.

The Saturday started out, as many of the previous mornings had weather wise, with a wind blowing. However, rather than be concerned about it, as I might be if I had plans at home, I had come to realise, that as at night, the temperature changes and according to Kevin, the tidal changes, causes the wind to alter throughout the day and so I knew that in a few hours it would be another fabulous day in the Bahamas. It had been an especially hot night and even with the ceiling fan going all night, I had had a much more disturbed nights sleep than normal. There is an air conditioning unit next to my bed, as mentioned earlier in the book, but that was far too noisy for me and was only turned on as I'm preparing for bed, once in bed, Vee would then turn it off. I was substituting a cool room for a quiet one and I pick quiet over cool every time.

I had just finished my hot water breakfast and was reading in my screened in veranda, when Kevin and Vee arrived and took me to the house known as 'High View'. This, as stated before, was so named because it was situated as the highest of the houses and offered some wonderful views! I decided to just sunbathe and positioned myself so that as much of my back as possible was facing the sun. I say as much of my back, because whilst sat in a wheelchair, the backrest is a natural barrier. Normally at home when sunbathing my back, there is a line where the top of the backrest has blocked out the sun, it's usually just below my shoulder blades. In the chair I'm in at the moment, the backrest is slightly lower and so, by leaning forward slightly, I can move the line further down. It's not a very comfortable position though, so I'm turning myself around every few minutes, alternating between leaning forward, to sun my back, to leaning as far back as I can to do my front, something like a chicken on a spit- roast. By 11.00 am I began to feel as though I was a chicken on a spit-roast and as Audrey was working in the kitchen of the house I was in, I asked her if I could be brought in to sit somewhere cooler. She helped me in, pushing the chair to the rear of the house, where there was a screened porch that faced to the East and therefore had the breeze pretty much continuously blowing through it. It was the ideal spot for me to cool down in and getting my journal out, I brought it up to date.

At around 11.45, Vee joined me for a while, which was a pleasant surprise and broke the silence a bit. She had just found out, via the Internet, that the football team she supports, Leeds United, had just won their game, which of course put her in a very good mood. Knowing also that I would be interested in hearing how my mate's team, Torquay had got on, she had looked that up and told me they had lost 5-3. Poor Bob I thought, I decided I must give him a ring on Monday, the night we usually met up for a beer and a chat to console him. For as long as I have known Bob, I have watched him go through the annual agony that numerous supporters must endure. When the team they watch and have supported, for many since childhood, are struggling to survive in the lower divisions. Bob greeted each win with hope and each loss with despair and a resignation that his much beloved team were destined for relegation. Vee and I had a good time together, chatting over all things football and sport in general, before she left for a stroll ahead of lunch.

Over lunch we discussed the plans for the afternoon. It was to be a boat trip to an island called Samson Cay, where Kevin needed to get some fuel. Apparently, the fuel tank they had on Soldier Cay, had sprung a leak and it required a skilled welder to come one day and fix it. In the mean time, they were using jerry cans and it was these we would be taking to refill. There was a bill he needed to pay as well, which meant that whilst he was doing that, Vee and I could have a quick stroll around and then once done, we would head back to pick up Audrey and finish the day snorkelling at the 'Aquarium'.

By 2.00 pm we were in the 'Carina', the speedboat, surrounded by jerry cans and setting off over again, the beautiful colours of the ocean. The thirty or so minute journey was a delight and once moored up and off the boat, Vee and I left Kevin to the task in hand whilst we explored the island. Sampson Cay was not a large island, a good-sized harbour, the refuelling station, a shop and a bar made up the most of it. We strolled around the harbour first, looking at the several large and very expensive looking yachts and motorboats all lined up, and then made our way into the shop. It was a shop that appeared to sell everything, clothes, food and other general items. We neither of us bought anything, nor needed too, we were just passing the time before heading off to the bar for a cooling drink. Halfway through our drink, Kevin joined us, telling us that all was done and after he allowed me to buy him a soft drink, we set off back to Soldier Cay, to pick up Audrey. It had been a pleasant time off Soldier Cay, a break from the routine of life there, but one of the strangest things about the hour, had been seeing people milling about. True, there had been only a half dozen or so, but after the near solitude of Soldier Cay, it nevertheless was a strange sensation.

We were once more mooring ourselves to the buoy at the 'Aquarium' and I was really ready for the water, almost excited about what I was soon to be doing and seeing. I had grown in confidence about the process of getting into the sea, aware that I was not about to drown due to the care and caution shown to me from Kevin and Audrey. I even felt bold enough to suggest to Kevin, that rather than going through the difficulty of lowering me into the water, why didn't he simply drop me in! I knew the flotation jacket would do it's job and get me to the surface should I go under and that Audrey would quickly get to me and put me on my back ready for the mask to be fitted, so why not? Kevin though, stuck with the safer option and as I was being lowered down, I realised that my being over confident was, in all probability, only due to the 7% extra strong 'Kalik' lager I had drunk, on an empty stomach, back at 'Sampson Cay'! Whatever, once in the water I was very quickly calm, warm and extremely relaxed and I really enjoyed that particular session!

By around 5 pm, we had all had a good period of snorkelling and as I was still in a happy and relaxed state, tipsy you might say, I asked if I could have a lazy swim off the Marina beach. This I was able to do and I found that the temperature there in the shallow water, was just perfect for me to relax in. After swimming about for a while, exercising my arms and shoulders, I simply stopped and floated about in a world of my own. I was loathed to move away from that spot. I so much wanted to hold onto the moment and the wondrous feeling I had and so rather than leave after getting out of the water, Kevin sat me on one of the plastic patio chairs at the top of the beach and I closed my eyes, luxuriating in the still warm sun, which by now, was slowly beginning to head for the far distant horizon.

It felt so unreal; I could still hardly believe that even after being there for over a week that this was true and happening to me. It felt like the stuff films were made of and I cried. I'm the sort of guy who will openly admit to crying at the end of a sad movie or book and as I looked about me, trying to absorb every last second of this day, another full and wonderful day, I thanked my lucky stars and felt the tears running down my face. They were tears of happiness and thankfulness and as I sat there, knowing that even though I could not feel the sand beneath my feet, I could feel so much more despite my disability, a condition that for this very moment was forgotten and something of little importance. I watched as my tears fell from my face down into the sand and felt a deep connection with what I physically could not feel, in that simple act.

Time was against me though and after 15 minutes or so, I was taken back to my home for a shower and to be dressed for the evening. And what an evening it would turn out to be, the perfect end to yet another perfect day.

The meal was shrimp and scallops in a wonderful sauce, served on a bed of pasta, accompanied with a glass or three of wine. After a short chat, giving our meals time to settle, Kevin then suggested we went through to their living room. But instead of stopping there, he carried on pushing me until we were outside on their veranda at the back of the house, saying, that it was a still and clear evening, ideal for stargazing.

Kevin positioned a lounger into some space and then tipped my chair back onto it until it was resting firmly. Then Audrey got a few of their scatter cushions and put them under the back of my head until I was comfortable. Once that was done, all the outside lights were turned off and we were submersed into total darkness. It took a few seconds for my eyes to adjust, but once they had, the view that greeted me was awesome. As I have said previously, there were more stars visible, even to the naked eye, than I have ever seen before and in the few moments I had glimpsed up whilst travelling to and from the houses in the evening, I had been transfixed. But now, as I lay there, I had the time and comfort to really look. At first I was a little disappointed, as there appeared to be some cloud in the way, even though Kevin had said it was a clear evening. But Audrey, passing me a pair of binoculars, said look again. It was only then, with the aid of the extra magnification that I realised, that though it was cloud of a sort that I was seeing, it was no cloud that surrounded this planet! It was the cloud, or whatever material, me being no expert on the night sky or astronomy, that made up the visible arm of the 'Milky Way' and the more intently I looked, the further I could see and the more I saw. It truly was a breathtaking moment for me, a definite wow time.

I spent 30 minutes in that position and they were all of them enjoyed. With or without the binoculars I could see so much. In fact, without them, I saw two shooting stars go flashing bye.

I was in bed by 10.30 pm, pretty much exhausted I reckon and my mind was awash with images of things I had seen and done. Sleep must have come quickly, for I don't remember much after that, other than Vee's cheery good morning, announcing the arrival of a new day, Sunday August the 16th 2009.

Day 11.

I have been a Christian since 1985 and have gained great comfort in my faith and belief in God. My wife and I both feel how important it is to start each day with some time of peace and reflection, saying a prayer or two in readiness for the day. Church for us is where ever we are and at whatever time of the day or week it may be, not just on a Sunday. For us it's when the moment feels right to say thank you. Church for me on this particular morning and not because it was a Sunday, was as usual, on my veranda with my hot water breakfast and whilst I looked again at the view from where I sat, I prayed my prayers of thanks, for all that had gone before and for the unknown adventures that still lay ahead.

Kevin appeared with a few tools and quickly sorted out a problem with my toilet. He then sat with me with a drink and after a general chat, once more got around to what the plan was for the day. He started by asking me if I wanted the bad news or the good news first? I said bad! He carried on, saying that this afternoon I was having a scuba lesson! At first my brain took on board the fact that he had said a snorkel lesson and I though, well, so what, I have already done that and so asked him what the good news was? He said that this afternoon I was having a scuba lesson! Then it struck me. Scuba, as in scuba diving, as in going under water, breathing with a tank strapped to your back scuba diving! The surprise look on my face brought a smile to Kevin's and before I could convince myself that this was not a very good idea, he began to carefully explain the plan of action, as he had with the snorkelling, once again making it sound a lot simpler than my brain was telling me right at this moment.

Whilst we were still chatting, having moved, very wisely, off the topic of being under water, Vee arrived. Between them they took me to the house next door to mine, the 'Runaway'. This is the house where Cecile, the owner's wife, does her thinking and writing. It was my turn to sit here, on my journey around the houses of the island, so that I could chill for a few hours before lunch and the afternoon's adventure. Only chill isn't the right word, as once again, now that the early morning breeze has eased, it's another hot day and I'm constantly on the move from the sun into the shade, barely able to enjoy the high temperature. The problem is, that because the breeze has dropped so much, the shade offers little respite from the heat, there's no air and it's almost as stifling as being in the sun. However, I'm able to take some pleasure from my time on my own there and soon enough Kevin and Vee reappear and we all go to Kevin's home for lunch, which for me today is a fruit smoothie.

I fancied having a chat with my wife and that is soon organised and when Ilona hears my voice she sounds relieved. She is fed up and lonely she say's, which is normal for Ilona sadly whenever I go away. She has never been able to relax or enjoy her own company, as I can when she goes on her break, but after five minutes she sounds a little happier and I hang up happy in the knowledge that she doesn't feel so completely on her own.

At around 2.20 pm we head off for Tikki Beach and whilst Kevin gets the rest of the equipment arranged, Audrey goes through with both Vee and myself, some basics about the tank. She explains as much as she can about the hoses and the mouthpiece, or regulator as it should be referred too, giving me a quick go at breathing with one. Everything seems to be ok and I'm fairly relaxed about things, until that is, as we near the time to go down to the water, a shark swims past us, very close to the beach! Kevin reassures me that it's only a nurse shark and perfectly harmless, but even so, I wait until I can no longer see it before agreeing to go in. I have my flotation jacket already on and once in the water, Kevin puts my mask and mouthpiece in place and turns me over. Almost immediately the mouthpiece shifts. My bite on the mouthpiece must be wrong, maybe due to my slightly misshapen gums, brought about by my being born with a double hair lip and cleft palate. Whatever, I'm no longer happy with the position of the mouthpiece and so I give the signal, a shake of my head, to alert Kevin that something is wrong and he turns me over.

After talking through the problem and also explaining to him how I had felt the buoyancy of the hose coming to me, as well as my poor grip, had pulled at the mouthpiece, Kevin repositions everything and suggests that I hold the regulator in place with my right hand and once I'm happy we try again. Success and after taking several breaths, Kevin turns me over again to give me further encouragement and asks that I take slower and shallower breaths. I then try this and yes it does feel more comfortable. I then see by the moving sand below me, that Kevin is once again, as he did when I first snorkelled, taking me to the dock to view the fish there and to be out in deeper water, giving me an extended view forward.

The obvious difference, I notice straight away, between snorkelling and using the scuba equipment is, that you are no longer restricted in where you can look. To continue breathing with the snorkel, you have to look down more than forward otherwise water will run into the pipe. With the mouthpiece of the scuba, you are free to turn your head where ever you want, which, once at the dock I did and what a difference. I could see so much further and consequently so much more.

Kevin was well pleased with my progress and figured I had done enough for the day, so we headed back to the beach and out. The first thing I felt, after the glow of having done something remarkable, for me anyway, had waned, was a bloated feeling in my chest and stomach. I must have been doing something wrong and had swallowed a lot of air and it took a while and several loud and embarrassing belches before the discomfort left.

I was dressed and ready for the evening a lot earlier than usual because the plan for this night was different from previous. Different as in we were having a meaty meal! Vee had told me and I had told Audrey prior to our coming over that she, Vee, was a vegetarian and so every night up to this, Audrey had done us all a vegetarian meal. It had been agreed though, that this night would be a red meat meal of some description and that Vee would have a separate meal on her own in the Beach House, in the company of a couple of DVD's of her choosing. We too were going to watch a couple of films, so it being the first time in over a week I had even been in front of a TV, this really was an altogether different evening.

The first film we watched was 'The Illusionist' and it wasn't a bad film at all. We then had our meal, which was a real treat and a surprise for me, shepherds pie! Several days ago, Audrey, whilst we were having a general chat about diet and likes and dislikes, had asked me what my all time favourite meal would be and without hesitation, I had told her shepherds pie. I have always found it to be, though a simple meal, one that has given me great pleasure and satisfaction and there it was in front of me. Now every meal that we had had these past several days, had been tasty and very enjoyable and I have gone to great lengths in describing them, simply because, as much as snorkelling or scuba diving had been an enjoyable experience, so was the evening meal. Having had nothing to eat all day, apart from a very simple lunch, the evening shared by us all was also something I looked forward too, hence my waxing lyrical over every meal. But this, because it had been prepared with me in mind, was extra special and to show my appreciation I had seconds! Kevin produced a superb bottle of red wine to accompany the meal, which also went down a treat. After the meal we finished off the evening by watching our second movie, 'Taken', which turned out to be a very predictable, but nevertheless entertaining action film.

By the time I got back to the Beach House, Vee had just finished watching her second film, making it perfect timing and within twenty minutes or so I had brushed my teeth, gone to the toilet and was tucked up in bed. I can't remember how long I had been asleep, but a passing storm woke me for a short while, before I eventually drifted off again.

Day 12.

It's Monday and instead of thinking about work to be done, reports to be read and meetings to attend, I'm sitting on my veranda reading the temperature gauge, which at 8.45 am, is already showing it to be at 31 degrees Celsius! It's going to be another hot day. I have time to finish off my 'Lee Childs' book, bring my journal up to date and get through most of the hot water left by Vee, before Kevin and Audrey arrive. Audrey is collecting the meal tray that Vee was given last night and something has upset her. It was the first time I had seen Audrey bothered by anything and I found out later that it was the fact that Vee had left half of the meal she had prepared for her and was upset at the apparent waste. It transpired later, that Vee had simply been full and whilst not wanting to cause offence, could eat no more. Kevin in the meantime was briefing me about today's adventures, which were to start at 10.00.

A little after 10.00, Kevin and Vee arrive and by 10.30, all four of us, including the two dogs, Tassel and Gizmo, are aboard the skiff heading off on the short boat ride to a nearby island called 'Osprey Cay'. The MacTaggart family also owns this island; in fact, Sandy bought it as a Christmas gift for his wife Cecile for two reasons. The first was so that no one else could buy it and so encroach on their privacy, it being as mentioned, fairly close and the second reason was to preserve it as a sanctuary and a safe haven for the Osprey that nested there, hence the name. It was a lot smaller than Soldier Cay, basically just a beach; with at one end a rocky outcrop where the nest could be seen, though empty at the moment. There are no buildings on the island and the family use it, when no ospreys are using the nest, as a picnic place. As we drew nearer to it, Kevin asks me if I have ever been marooned on an island before! Now, whilst I have always though I could survive, like Robinson Crusoe, totally alone on a desert island, I have never had the chance to try it out, that is, until today!

Kevin is telling me that the plan is, to drop me off at one end of the island, the beach end, then motor away for half an hour or so and anchor the boat at the other end. Then, using his home made beach-crossing chair, the one I use to gain access into the sea, which is in the skiff with us, rescue me and wheel me back along the beach. This sounds fun I think and before long I'm sitting on the beach in a patio chair, with a bottle of water in my hand, watching the others move away into the far distance. I am literally on my own and apart from the noise of the lapping waves just a few yards to my right, there is neither a sound nor another living thing around me. It's a glorious sensation, total isolation, peace and beauty all around me and how and why I didn't cry again is beyond me.

After what seemed only a short while, but must have been nearer an hour, I see two figures, Kevin, pushing his home made chair and Audrey coming my way. Vee must be exploring the rest of the island, because she's not in sight and the two dogs are doing what dogs do, sniffing and playing, just behind the pair who are getting closer and closer.

After a photo shoot of me in my patio chair, Kevin transfers me and starts to push me back from where they have just come and Audrey drags the patio chair behind her. We stop a couple of times on the way for a rest and to look at and pick as souvenirs, some shells, one of which is a conch shell, that now sits proudly in my living room, next to my fish tank.

Once back near the rocky outcrop, we all cool down with a welcome drink and Audrey begins to tell me a little more about island life. She explains, that even though, as an owner of a private island, you make think yourself free from intrusion, in reality the law say's differently. She then points to a point further up the beach, to where the high tide mark is, a visible line of leaves and other debris that had been left by the incoming tide. She goes on to say to me, that anyone could, if they had a mind to, come onto your island and picnic or do pretty much whatever they wanted to, as long as they encroached no further on to your island than the high tide mark! This came as quite a surprise to me and I asked if people actually did that? Audrey said that people have tried it on Soldier Cay, but added, that the sight of Kevin, who is a large very well built man, loitering nearby with a shotgun soon sent them packing!

After sitting there chatting for half an hour or so and again having some photo's taken, we pack up our things, making sure we leave the place as clean and tidy as it was when we arrived. In fact it's even cleaner, as Vee, on her walk around, had picked up a plastic bottle that had been washed ashore and put it with the things we were taking back to dispose of. Once back in Kevin and Audrey's kitchen, I have a bowl of cornflakes for lunch and after phoning my mate Bob for a quick chat, consoling him over his teams poor performance on the Saturday, I sit outside on their veranda for a while, enjoying the hot sun. I'm looking at the temperature gauge hanging near their back door and it's showing to be once more in the mid thirties, proving my thinking earlier right about it going to be another hot day. This then makes it all just about perfect for me to relax for a while, before we head off later in the afternoon to the 'Aquarium' for my second scuba diving session.

At around 4.00 pm we are again moored up at the 'Aquarium' and Kevin, whilst he helps me put my flotation jacket on, is telling me that if all goes well, he will be taking me down just two or three feet. This will give me an idea, he says, the sensation of being under water and not floating, as before, on top of it. Once safely in and breathing quite happily, I feel Kevin putting some ballast, some lead weights into the pockets of the jacket to get me below the surface. Now when I was in the army and swimming with the lads, I was picked out as one of the sinkers, someone who naturally sinks to the bottom because of my build. So when later, Kevin told me that he loaded me with 14lb of ballast before I began to go under, it made me smile, how times change. Anyway, I'm under the water and the whole experience is a lot different from being on top. I'm looking around seeing a little more as we move around the 'Aquarium', when suddenly I feel my feet brush against something! Now my paralysis is not complete, so there is some slight feeling in all areas below the level of my injury, namely from my collarbones down. But I'm not too sure what it is I'm touching, so, I look down and notice with a little alarm, but no real panic, that my feet are touching the bottom! I'm almost sitting on the bottom of the twenty-foot deep 'Aquarium'! So much for Kevin's assurances of how things were going to be for the afternoon, or maybe he planned it that way? Anyway, he told me later, that he saw no alarm or concern from me and so took the plunge so to speak. Whatever, I'm glad, for I'm doing this for real I realised, not just paddling around in the learner pool, I'm twenty feet under looking at the many amazing sights all around me. There is the myriad of different fish swimming around me and above me. I'm gently moving my hands through the plant life that's growing in abundance and looking at the many different colours of the coral. It's an awesome sight and an awesome feeling, another definite wow moment. The best 25 minutes so far!

My having a shower and getting changed for the evening back at the Beach House was a blur, as my thoughts were constantly flitting from one event to another of the day. Being marooned on a desert island was great, diving twenty feet at the aquarium was great, how on earth I thought, could things get much better than this? Well apparently they could!

My thoughts are a little more together by the time I'm sitting around the dining table with the others. It's another fabulous meal, Mahi Mahi, a fish I have never even heard of before, on a bed of cus cus with spaghetti and squash, as in the vegetable. This is followed by ice cream, washed down with another tasty wine, whilst all the while we are chatting about the day and whatever else comes to mind.

By the end, it's quite a late evening for me, compared to the other nights; but I don't feel as tired as usual, even though I have had yet another extraordinary and full day and once more I fall asleep quickly, with the thoughts, memories and experiences of the day, filling my mind.

Day 13.

My night was again disturbed by a storm. It's getting close to the season of hurricanes and storms, which officially goes from June 1st until the end of November, but is at it's potential worst, from September through October and I'm hoping that my last few days here are not spoilt by any drastic change in the weather. It would be totally the wrong memory for me to go home with. Kevin, who has just left me, after staying and talking me through the plan for today and chatting for 45 minutes, has informed me that the storm in the night was the tail end of a tropical storm named Anna. Apparently all severe storms and hurricanes are given a name and Anna came relatively close to us. Close enough, Kevin said, to give him some concern. He has one ear on the radio for more weather alerts and has started the laborious job of sorting out the storm screens that each house has, that will need to be fastened to the windows during this season. However, he is confident, based on his experience gained over the years out in these conditions that nothing too serious is about to happen just yet and my few remaining days should go on ok and without too much trouble. Within a few minutes of him leaving, the wind begins to fade and his assertions seem to be bearing out and I'm more than hopeful for another pleasant day.

At 11.20 am I'm picked up and we head off for the marina. Once we are all in the skiff, we head of for the sandbank, which is literally just a couple of hundred yards away for 'The Photograph'!

I have mentioned several times already, how in preparing for this trip, Audrey and I kept in touch via email. We chatted about a great many things. From what to pack and what not to, how the initial first few days would be organised, to the various timings leading up to being met by Kevin at the airport. A long list of things based on various questions I was asking of them and they were asking of me and with a few of the answers came, 'teaser photo's' as Audrey called them. Pictures showing snippets of the island, their dogs and their home. One of the photographs I received, was of Audrey swimming in a few inches of sea, just off what looked like to me, a beach and in the distance you could see the white roofs of a couple of the houses on the island. The colour of the water she was in and the whiteness of the sand in the photograph were stunning; I truly had never seen anything like it in my life. It was a photograph that summed up all that I wanted to do during my stay. Never realising at the time that I would go on to do much more than just swim in the sea. Anyway, in my reply to that email and picture, I asked that if I do nothing else, could I have a photograph taken of me in that exact same spot. It turned out, once I had arrived and settled and discussions turned around to actually having the picture taken, that the beach I thought I saw in the original photo, was in fact a sandbank that appeared twice a day when the tide went out. Once safely anchored then near the sandbank, the patio chair is taken off and then I'm lifted out and put in the chair. Next I'm lifted up again and sat on the sand with my legs out straight in front of me and my arms locked straight behind my back supporting myself. With a part of my body with which I could feel normal contact, my hands, now in direct touch with the sand, I could feel the fine grains and could also feel them sinking slowly into the still wet white sand. I'm now looking at the exact same view I saw in their original photo. This was it for me, the moment, even after all the wonderful moments I had enjoyed so far, this was the one that defined what the holiday was about and this time nothing could stop the tears from falling. If that wasn't a glorious enough moment for me, then it got better, when Kevin appeared in my view holding a very nice bottle of chilled 'Veuve Clicquot Champagne'.

As part of the conversation a few nights ago about my all time favourite meal, my love of Champagne had been highlighted as my all time favourite drink, which was true. I have loved Champagne ever since buying my first bottle for my parents wedding anniversary when I was around eighteen years old and have since drunk it at every opportunity offered to me. Anyway, the bottle Kevin was holding, with its famous yellow label, was quickly opened, glasses were produced and toasts were made to a fabulous and memorable holiday. So, I'm sat on the sandbank, that is only ten or fifteen yards wide, by about thirty yards long, surrounded by the sea, sipping Champagne and thinking about how many times in this break so far, have I thought to myself, can it get any better than this and I decide in that moment to give up wondering if it can. It has felt to me that each new day has brought new and more wondrous adventures and rather than contemplate on if things can indeed get any better, I decide to simply enjoy each new moment.

Audrey was in her element with the camera, taking quite a few of me on my own, then taking group photos. These, as had been the case every night, would be shown me on their computer later. I can honestly say, as we scanned through them later, that when I saw the one of me that was taken from behind, showing the Champagne to my right and the exact same view I had seen in the photograph of Audrey, sent me many months before coming over, I said without hesitation, that that was the one picture, out of all the many Audrey had taken, that defined the holiday, it was 'The Photograph'.

The tide began slowly creeping in after sitting there for fifteen minutes or so and I notice how the waves are getting closer and closer to my feet. So I'm lifted up and put back in the patio chair to finish off the Champagne and to carry on enjoying the moment. It has only been an hour since we left the marina, but what an hour. The skiff is made ready and sadly we have to leave, heading back to Kevin and Audrey's veranda for lunch.

Lunch is delayed slightly, because Kevin announces that there is to be a presentation! He disappears for a few seconds, returning with a beautifully framed certificate. It's a PADI certificate, (Professional Association of Diving Instructors) with scroll writing and a gold seal, certifying that Mr. Steve Rigby has satisfactorily completed a sanctioned course in scuba diving. It even has a photograph on it, showing the moment Kevin and I surfaced after the dive at the 'Aquarium'. It's fabulous and touching, because after that dive, as I was being dried on the boat, I had jokingly said, did I get a certificate for that. Kevin had said he would sort it out, but I thought he, as I had, had been joking and had thought nothing more of it until today. Apparently he had phoned the head office of PADI in the U.S.A. and asked if it was ok to award it and they had given him the go ahead. He had then spent some time putting one together, frame and all and I just knew, as I held it and admired it, that it would hang proudly somewhere where it could be seen and enjoyed, which I'm pleased to say it does.

The rest of the afternoon is given to relaxing, with a swim planned for around 4.00 pm. But when the time comes and Kevin asks what did I fancy doing, I look outside and notice that the wind has picked up considerably and the waves that I can see from where I'm sitting, look choppy. On the basis of how much cooler and a lot less enjoyable it is likely to be because of the wind, I decide to stay put and forgo my swim. I intend to just hang around where I am until 6.00 pm, when Vee would come to get me ready for the evening. My thinking is, that having a swim, getting wet and cold, as nice as it has been in the past, would not be enjoyable and ultimately would have spoilt some great memories of the day.

Just before 6.00, Vee arrives and even with having a shower, has a hard job getting all the sand off me. It's in every crevice of my body and it appears some of it is coming home with me in a couple of days! Bearing in mind the cooler evening, I'm dressed in a long sleeved shirt and a light sweater, much to the amusement of Kevin and Audrey. However, I figure being dressed as I am will serve two purposes. One, to help ward off the bugs that are still feasting on my exposed arms and neck during the short drive home and secondly, the sky doesn't look too great, hurricane Anna is still showing itself and there's a feeling of rain in the air and the extra layers will hopefully keep me dry and warm.

Supper that evening was a BBQ cooked perfectly by Kevin, sadly though, as I suspected, the heavens opened and the rain forced us to enjoy our meal indoors. Thankfully it didn't spoil our time together, with lots to talk about and share, after yet another exciting day.

Day 14.

It's Wednesday the 19th of August and as I drink my hot water, I sadly acknowledge the fact that it is my last full day here on Soldier Cay. The weather is greatly improved, finally the storm has moved on and I intend to fully enjoy it, whatever it may bring, rather than thinking about packing and the journey home tomorrow.

Kevin has told me that he has planned a trip out in the motorboat for one last dive and if all goes well, a chance to have a final swim off the Marina beach. The birds and the Cicada beetles are particularly noisy today, it could be that they, like me, are relieved that the storm has moved on. I have to say, that of all the many different things that I have experienced these past fourteen days, the noise from these creatures has been the one constant. Perhaps not always as loud as they are today, or maybe I, like Kevin and Audrey, had grown used to them and learnt how to block them out, whatever, they are back in my mind with a vengeance right at this moment and I'm looking forward to our trip away from them later on.

At 10.45 am, Vee joins me and we have a chat about the holiday whilst waiting for Kevin. We both agree how awesome the whole experience has been, how long the two weeks have felt and how strange it was going to be getting back to our normal lives at home and mingling back into the cut and thrust of civilisation. But in thinking about that conversation later on, I realised that I was actually looking forward to being back home and yes, even mingling back into civilisation. I had, soon after arriving and settling in, thought how fabulous the quiet and the isolation was. But now, as the holiday neared the end, I thought how lonely it was, too quiet even for me and I marvelled at how Kevin and Audrey had coped with their solitary kind of life all this time. So perhaps, unlike Robinson Crusoe, I might well struggle after all, having to live on my own on a desert island?

When Kevin arrives a few minutes later, he has with him yet another certificate for my scuba diving exploits. It appears that following on from his phone conversation with the PADI office in the U.S.A., to ask if I could be awarded a certificate, as well as the one Kevin organised, they too had sent one over. It's a certificate announcing that I had participated in a special programme of scuba diving and once I had this one framed back home a few weeks later, in as similar a style as my first, it meant that the two could hang side by side in my Pride Park office in Derby. I asked if I could have some photographs taken of me receiving the original one and Kevin suggested that they could be taken at the marina after lunch, before we head off for our final dive.

Lunch for me was a piece of toast with grilled cheese, then at 1.00 pm we set off for the marina and the photographs of the framed certificate. Once several had been taken, then came the job of getting me into the Carina, the motorboat. I say 'the job', because from where I'm sitting on the dock of the marina, I can clearly see that the tide must be out, because the deck of the Carina is easily four feet below the level of the dock and I express some doubt as to Kevin's ability to get me in! Now, after all that I have done, thanks in the main to the ingenuity and strength of both Kevin and Audrey, I should have known better than to doubt them now. I suppose I was expressing my fear for all our safety, because the very last thing I wanted was to be the cause of some mishap in trying, what appeared to me, something beyond even Kevin's ability. How wrong I was and once again how easy the two of them made it appear, almost as if they did this sort of thing every day. Kevin ticked me off, in a light hearted way for doubting him and repeated his well used phrase to me during this time with them, saying, that the word impossible was not a word in his vocabulary. I had pretty much come to believe it by now and vowed never to use it again in any circumstance. We were all safely aboard anyway and setting off for a dive location known as 'Jeep Reef', which according to Kevin, is one of the top thirty dives in the world and bearing in mind his knowledge and experience, I don't doubt it.

A small buoy anchored to the seabed marks this location, as was the case when we went to feed the sharks, which again was hard to find because of the swell of the ocean. Eventually though, Audrey spotted it and a few minutes later we were fastened to it and preparing for the dive. Kevin pointed out that this was a little deeper than our previous dive at the 'Aquarium' and said that if I feel any discomfort, meaning pressure on my ears, I should say so. But having had no difficulty so far, I thought it oughtn't to be a problem now. Once in the water, settled with my breathing and over the cold, we soon drop to the bottom for some spectacular sights. As this location is in a more open part of the sea, as apposed to the more or less enclosed 'Aquarium', the views are far more widespread. The sea is still clear, giving near perfect vision in every direction. Kevin, who is turning me around to catch a glimpse of the sea life I have only ever seen before on T.V, is giving me the grand tour. There is a problem after a while though. It must be due of the extra depth we are at, because there is a small amount of pain developing in my ears, but more troublesome than that, is the pressure on my head and face from the mask. It's beginning to squeeze quite hard and I'm getting a slight headache. I'm loathed to give the distress signal to Kevin though, regardless of the pain, I'm enjoying this too much to stop and I soldier on. I was to be reminded by Kevin later, when I had confessed about my discomfort, that all I had to do to alleviate the pain, was to equalise the pressure in the mask by breathing out through my nose a couple of times. An apparently simple solution and one I vowed to remember should there ever be a next time.

Soon enough we approach the surface and once more Audrey and her camera greet us. The mask is pulled off and I breathe a quiet sigh of relief. I'm grinning so much, one because of the immediate loss of pain in my head and secondly, because that was the most amazing time I have ever experienced. I know I have said that several times already, but it was true, an experience to cap all before them and a perfect and fitting end to my two weeks. As I lay on my back on the padded seating area at the stern of the Carina, my lower legs still dangling over the end, I feel the warmth of the sun on my body and a feeling of euphoria sweeps over me. My eyes are closed and a joke about scuba diving comes to mind and it's one I feel compelled to share out loud. It's the story of two elderly men sitting on their deck chairs on the sea front. They are enjoying the sunshine and the views all around them. After a while, their gaze turns to a boat in the near distance, where two people on the boat are readying themselves to go scuba diving. After the splash of their entry into the sea has faded and the divers have disappeared, one old man turns to the other and asks; "Why do divers jump into the sea backwards"? Without hesitation, the other man reply's, "don't be silly, if they jumped forwards they would land in the boat"! My efforts at humour are rewarded with a groan and a laugh from my captive audience and with that, I'm placed into my chair and given a towel to dry off with.

Next to have a dive is Vee who is being helped on with all the equipment. She was invited to have a go and I was pleased to hear that she agreed. She had participated with pretty much everything I had done thus far and it would have been a shame for her to miss out on such an opportunity as this. Audrey is diving with her and within a few minutes they disappear. Whilst I enjoy the early afternoon sun on my face, Kevin sorts out the equipment we used and generally gets the boat ready for our return trip home. We chat and talk more about our respective army days and after about twenty minutes, Vee and Audrey surface and Kevin helps them out. He asks Vee if she enjoyed herself and with a grin on her face as big as mine had been, she expresses herself in the only way she said she was able to at the time, because, she said later, she was lost for words, by swearing. Not the language I had heard her use before, but they were nevertheless, words that clearly expressed her pleasure at her time under water.

It's only 3.00 pm when we arrive back at Soldier Cay, so we make our way to the Marina beach for one final swim, a swim that nearly turned into my last one ever!

I'm soon in the still warm water and floating around, paddling with my arms occasionally to keep me in line with the beach and in view of Audrey and Vee. I then exercise my arms by moving them around backwards and forwards under the water, pushing hard against it's resistance, knowing that this truly is my last opportunity to enjoy the sheer pleasure of this moment for heaven knows how long. Then I have a rest and float about for a while, closing my eyes and enjoying the sensation of the warmth from the sun and the feeling of being carried by the buoyancy of the water. Carried being the operative word, because I'm suddenly aware that Audrey has grabbed hold of the float under my neck and is trying to pull me backwards. That was quite ironic I thought later, she being an ex policewoman, feeling my collar so to speak. Anyway, unbeknown to me, whilst I had my eyes closed and was relaxing, I had drifted into the tidal flow and was fast disappearing from view! Vee told me later, that she had seen me and thought I must be ok and had casually asked Audrey if she thought I was all right where I was. Audrey realising that in fact all was not well, had swum after me

112

and was now trying to pull me back against the tide. She was struggling with this and eventually had to alert Kevin, who, laughing at my predicament, had to fetch one of the boats and tow the both of us in to shore. Through his tears of laughter, he reckoned that at the speed I was going at, I would have been in Cuba by nightfall and with that, came the end of my adventures, but thankfully, not quite the end of my holiday.

The early finish to the day's activities, meant that after my shower and then being dressed, I was at Kevin and Audrey's home earlier too. This was ok with me, as it was going to allow us all a more leisurely night; fitting I thought, as it was the last one.

Sitting in their living room at around 6.00 pm, with some background music playing softly, a cold drink on my lap and a bowl of peanuts to hand, we chatted about the day. Having a laugh at my expense over my attempts to swim to Cuba, which was fine with me and also sharing a few thoughts about how next time, things could be improved upon. I had as yet not dared to ask if, all being well, I could come again, however, it seemed that this was indeed a possibility and that pleased me enormously. So this was a conversation I had hoped would come up on it's own, without me jumping in with my hopes for the future years and the possible breaks with them. The future months and our emails to and from would soon sort the possibility of repeating this wonderful time out and so I didn't pursue the conversation too vigorously.

It was then time to go through to the dining room for our meal, which tonight was a medley of fish with a mixed layered bowl of vegetables as an accompaniment. Sitting proudly as the top layer of vegetables of the bowl, were

'Brussels Sprouts'! How on earth Audrey got them, I have yet to fathom, but I like sprouts so enjoyed them and as always, the meal as a whole. The background music that had been continually playing during the meal, naturally brought the conversation to musical tastes and amazingly, to me anyway, it transpired that both Vee and Audrey liked to listen to heavy rock music! That particular choice for them came as a complete surprise to me. I thought I had gotten to know them both a little better over these past two weeks, but I would never have put either of them down as fanciers of heavy rock. Audrey then asked Vee if she would enjoy listening to some CD's she had and they both went off to the sitting room. Neither Kevin nor I fancied the idea, not our cup of tea at all, so we contented ourselves with a little more catching up over our army days, whilst playing the best of three games of backgammon. I won 2-0, making it 2-2 in the series and we agreed that we would play the decider sometime the next morning, before our leaving. The mere mention of our leaving the next day, brought the evening, for me, to a sad close and by 9.50 pm, after brushing my teeth, I was tucked up in bed.

Day 15.

So this was it, Thursday and my last day. Whilst sitting in my usual morning spot, I'm aware that there is no breeze at all; it's one of the calmest and therefore hottest starts to the day there has been since arriving. The temperature gauge nearby is reading around 38 degrees Celsius and I'm dressed, or at least my lower half is, for the journey home, with trousers, socks and shoes. I had decided when I first woke up, that when Vee came in to get me up, rather than go through the dressing process twice, to get it done straight off, leaving just a shirt to put on last thing. I had made this choice, even though we are not due to leave the island until around 4.00 pm and that it left me more than ample time to perhaps swim or sunbathe. My thinking was though, that I knew I would not fully enjoy it, as my mind would be focussing on getting home and by being half ready, it forced me to think about that and not what I might be able to do in the waiting time. As I have said right at the beginning of this story, I'm terrible at waiting. I worry and stress over every aspect of a journey such as this and mooching around in my shorts up to the moment of leaving would simply churn me up. I have had ample time to swim and enough sun in these last fourteen days to turn my skin darker than even I can remember, so I'm content enough to wait partially dressed, even with this heat.

Kevin has dropped in for his early morning chat and has asked if I would like him to plant a baby palm tree in my honour and if so, where would I like it to go. Whilst I'm thinking about that, Vee appears with my Conch shell that Audrey has cleaned up and carefully wrapped and a CD she has produced of all the photographs she took with her camera. We three then chat about the timings for the day, which as I have said are planned to start at around 4.00

115

pm. The plans include, a last tour of the memorable spots on the island in the golf buggy and then as we leave, a boat tour around the island. Kevin and Vee then leave together, leaving me to finish off what packing I can do myself and to bring my journal as up to date as possible.

Just before 11.30, Kevin is back with the baby palm, which stands about two foot six inches tall and has three healthy leaves on it and by this time, I have decided where it should go. I have picked a spot just to the left of my favourite view, as seen from where I have sat every morning. This is so as not to spoil that same view for others, bearing in mind it will grow, hopefully, into quite a large tree and so that if and when I do come back, I will still have my view and sight of my tree. Kevin then sets too with digging a hole and once he has bedded it in, gives me the honour of watering it, using a hose he has connected up. He assures me that it should be ok and promises to take regular photographs of its progress, which he will then email too me.

Vee has joined us again and after loading me into the golf buggy, then my luggage, we set off on the farewell tour of the island. This movement on the buggy comes as a blessed relief, as it's so hot and there is still no breeze. We stop off at all the points on the island I spent time at, taking a few more pictures and then head off to Kevin and Audrey's for lunch and the chance to cool off in their air-conditioned kitchen. As with my journey here, I'm keeping my fluid and food intake down to the bear minimum to minimise the risk of my needing the toilet on the plane. This means, as it has throughout this holiday, that lunch for me is a simple meal, a small bowl of fruit salad. After lunch, whilst Vee goes back to hers to finish off her packing and to have a shower, Kevin and I play our deciding game of backgammon. He wins this match 2-0, which makes him the overall winner of all our matches 3-2. As we are not setting off till later in the afternoon, I then sit outside on their veranda, soaking up the sunshine for one last time, using the shade as and when needed.

The rest of the day, if all goes according to plan, is that at 3.30 pm we are all meeting up to start the homeward journey with a boat trip around the island, then it's off to Staniel Cay to catch the small plane back to Nassau. Audrey will be with us for the start of our homeward journey and has already intimated that we were having a meal in Nassau at a sensible time, rather than on the plane, which would mean having our meal sometime around midnight. We will then head off to the airport to check in and wait for our flight which is due to leave at 11.00 pm local time, or 4.00 am, as it would be back home, landing back in Heathrow around 11.30 am. Then hopefully, Charlie our taxi driver will already be at the airport, waiting to take us on our final leg home, north up the M1.

It's sadly soon 3.30 and we head off to the marina and get aboard the skiff for the last time. Our baggage is secured and we set off slowly, passing as close as possible, the main sights of the island. The last place we visit is the small bay where my home for the last twelve days, the Beach House, is located and with a little twinge of sadness, I say farewell as Kevin turns the skiff and we head off for Staniel Cay. It's a sometimes-bumpy journey over, especially in the more open areas of the sea, where the protection from the wind and waves is lessened when the gaps between the many islands that makes up the Exuma Chain is bigger. Not good for my tummy, bearing in mind the next time I will have the opportunity to visit a toilet, is many hours ahead! We arrive at our destination around 5.00 pm, just as the plane that is taking us back does and just as an enormous storm cloud rolls in with the first, as yet, gentle rain drops falling down upon us.

Mindful of how disruptive the storm could be to our plans, Kevin quickly secures the skiff and sorts out our getting to the plane. Once at the plane, getting in is as awkward as it was the first time, with me being dragged up the wing and into my seat. However, once settled, all is well and I'm in one piece, which is more than can be said for my wheelchair. They are having great difficulty removing one of the large wheels and it's only later, I realise, that the sand and salt water, combined with my several showers taken from the chair, has caused the spindle holding the wheel in place to rust slightly and it would take a visit to my home from my brother John a few weeks later, along with his tool box to sort it out. In the meantime the chair, already quite small and capable of folding at the back, is somehow squeezed into the luggage compartment along with all our bags and with an emotional farewell to Kevin, we lift off just as the heavier rain arrives.

We quickly fly through the rain clouds and are soon in clear and blue sky, enjoying once more the views below. All aboard the plane are quiet and subdued, perhaps aware, as I am, that this is the end of something truly remarkable and aware also that conversation would do nothing to lift our moods. This makes for a more difficult journey, one though in which I'm content enough to just look out of the window.

Touch down at Nassau is at around 5.45 pm and we are faced once more with problems with my wheelchair. The hammering they gave it in trying to load it, back at Staniel Cay, has meant that the one wheel that did eventually come off, now won't go back on fully into it's locked state. This means that every time I move and turn the chair, the spindle that holds the wheel in place moves out of it's seating, meaning, that if left un-noticed, the wheel would eventually fall off, which is not ideal under any circumstances! Audrey dispatches one of the ground crew in search of a toolbox, but whilst waiting, finds a suitably heavy rock with which to hit the locking pin with. So, whilst Vee helps to lean me and my chair over to one side, Audrey hits the locking pin enough to firmly secure the wheel and although my focus is constantly on it, checking to see that it has remained in place, nothing untoward happens and the wheels remain exactly where they are, until my brother intervenes.

We are met by the same driver and stretch limo that brought us to the airport and once loaded, a more difficult job this time because of the chair problem, we set off for the restaurant, 'The Poop Deck West' that Audrey eluded too earlier, for a meal. We are to meet up with their friends who we met at their home many days ago, Roy and Marilyn. They are joining us for the meal, as well as afterwards helping us to the airport and then once we were away, taking Audrey back home. Audrey insists on a nice table, which we get and as soon as our drinks arrive, so do Roy and Marilyn. After ordering, what I hoped was the lightest and easiest meal to digest; Roy produces a bag, which he presents to Vee. In it is a bottle of liquor that she has enjoyed whilst being in the Bahamas and a carton of cigarettes bought for her by them as a farewell gift. I neither drink liquor nor smoke, so had no intention of taking anything back, bought or given, as duty free goods. Nevertheless, once Vee had thanked them for the gift, Marilyn then produced a large padded envelope, which she proceeded to hand over to me. With a little help from Audrey in removing the sticky tape and then the contents, I was suddenly confronted with a canvass picture tacked around a wooden frame. The picture was the very same one that I had said defined the holiday for me, the one with me sat on the sandbank with the Champagne bottle and glass by my side. Audrey had obviously forwarded the photo to Roy, who had then gone to a place in Nassau that prints photos onto canvass, a popular gift idea I believe and one that I found very touching. It was a lovely thought and the picture now hangs right over my T.V. at home, so that at a glance, I can be transported back to that moment.

The meals then arrived and after carefully putting away our gifts, we eat our food, talking all the while about what we had all seen and done since we last met. It was again, a lovely time, fitting that it should be our last moment together and if Kevin had walked in at that moment, it would have capped off the whole two-week adventure.

By the time the meal is over and we reach the main departure point at the airport, my stomach is aching. As much I feel from the meal, as from the fact that this is it, we are about to say our final farewells, something we all find hard to do. We drop our bags off, are told, as 'Club World' passengers, where the business class lounge is situated and disappear from Audrey, Roy and Marilyn's sight, waving all the while. After rounding several corners, we find ourselves in a lounge area, but it doesn't have the look of an up graded lounge. However, we are both content just to sit for a while, in order to catch our breaths after the emotion of saying our goodbyes.

Once settled, Vee says she has to pop off to the toilet and giving me all our carry on bags, she wanders off. Upon her return she says that she has found the business class lounge and so we head off towards it and it is so much better. By the time Vee had got back, there had gathered all around me quite a noisy crowd of passengers, waiting, as we were, for flights and walking into the business class lounge was like entering a different place all together. Soft furnishings, drinks machines, a T.V. and only three other people sitting there. This made it a much quieter and more pleasant place to wait and as it was only 8.30 pm, it meant we had another two and a half hours to go, time better spent where we were, rather than in the noisy and crowded main lounge. So in the end then, I felt it really was well worth the extra cost involved in upgrading.

After organising some drinks for us both, Vee settled down into a comfy armchair with a magazine from the rack and her music, whilst I watched an old classic comedy film, 'Nuns on the Run' on the T.V. I know it very well, but I also know it will easily eat into the time remaining before boarding, reducing my stress levels somewhat. However, when the clock nearby is showing 10.30 pm, I begin to get a little agitated. As usual though, I was worrying about nothing, for a few minutes later someone drew near asking if my name was Rigby and after confirming it by showing our boarding tickets, he took hold of the wheelchair and pushed me through the departure lounge, to the head of the now growing queue of people all preparing to board. We quickly went through all the usual boarding checks and then my helper left me in the hands of others, who eventually get me into my seat on the plane. First of all though, I ensure that my wheelchair cushion is in place. It straightaway makes a huge difference. I'm higher in my seat for one thing, as well as having no discomfort what so ever and immediately I'm more relaxed, knowing that the next eight hours or so are not going to be as uncomfortable as the inward flight had been.

We take off pretty much on time and after toasting our holiday and our journey home with a glass of Champagne, Vee puts my feet up on the footstool and after checking that all of my tubes are still connected to me and are without any kinks to my leg bag, covers me with a blanket. We both settle down as best we can and decline the in-flight meal when offered it, it's midnight local time, far to late, as Audrey had said, to enjoy a meal.

As the rest of the passengers ready themselves for sleep and the cabin crew put things away in the overhead lockers and generally close the plane down for the night flight, I'm doing my best to get really comfortable and whilst sitting on my pressure relief cushion has worked, I'm still not able to fully relax and so the next six hours drag bye. There is, even for me, only so much T.V. I can watch and games of chess and backgammon I can play. So I try to doze, I close my eyes and allow my thoughts to wander over the past two weeks. I become fully alert suddenly though, when I realise that my leg bag is filling and in fact is pretty much full and I know from years of experience that should my bladder work one more time, my bag being full means I'm going to get wet! I lean across in the direction of Vee and in a voice intended to wake her only and not those nearby, try to rouse her from her sleep. By the third attempt, I'm also jabbing her shoulder and with what to me seems to be a startled or disgruntled look, she opens her eyes and as quickly as she can, in her half wake half sleep state, reaches for the urine bottle in my carry on bag and empties my leg bag for me. It was done in the nick of time too, for just as she closes the tap at the bottom of the bag, my bladder works again and starts to fill it once more. Once she's back in her seat, we both realise that we are only an hour away from landing and just as the cabin crew begin the process of offering hot face towels and drinks and preparing things in general for landing, so we ready ourselves.

We land as scheduled around 11.40 am and I'm tired but very relieved. Getting through baggage reclaim and customs again went without a hitch and as soon as we have found some space, close to where we had arranged to meet Charlie our taxi driver two weeks ago, I phone him. He picks up quickly and tells me he can see me through the crowd, which means that in only a few minutes, we are once more in his car and heading off on the final leg of this adventure, the journey home.

We are soon into the madness and chaos of the Friday afternoon motorway traffic around the M25 and because of some further traffic problems he was aware of, Charlie decides on an alternate route home, leaving the M25 and the M1 North to those more determined than we were. We were hopeful of getting back home around 4.00 pm, leaving me with ample time to contemplate on all that has happened to me, the new experiences I had gained and the new friendships.

As Charlie focussed on his driving and Vee relaxed on the back seat, I realised that I had learnt a huge amount about myself in terms of where my limits, both emotional and physical lay. Where I had thought they were previously, had been shifted forward miles and given the right people around me and the right encouragement, I now knew I could do so much more than I had ever thought possible. Kevin and Audrey had introduced me to a world where the words, I can't, don't exist. I had gained a great deal of satisfaction and pleasure from doing the many new things I had done, as well as a great deal of respect and love for all the people I had met and who had helped make the trip possible. Yes I had gained so many things from these two weeks, but what did I leave behind? Apart from my two pairs of shorts that were torn to tatters by the end, a few tears in the sand maybe!

So, as we neared home and my thoughts began to move on from my holiday too the more mundane, to my work and the busy and hectic life I lead, I realised, that despite the severity of my disability and because of all that I had experienced these past two weeks, my holiday of a lifetime, my adventure of a lifetime, wasn't at all drawing to a close. In fact, as I looked forward to the years that lay ahead and whatever else that might bring, with regard to my future holidays in the sun that I was now determined to take come what may, it dawned on me, that the adventure was only just beginning!

About The Author

Steven was born in the Potteries in November 1954, one of eight children, having five sisters and two other brothers.

He grew up with a passion for sport, having a natural ability that was to lead him on a path that was to eventually and dramatically change his life.

Educated at the Oldfields Secondary Modern School in Uttoxeter, he left having just turned 15 with no exam certificates to his name.

He started work as an apprentice upholsterer and carpet fitter, moving after five years to the local biscuit factory at the age of 20 to work in the engineering stores department.

Being unfulfilled, he decided to combine his passion for all things sport with his liking of the military, thanks to his time served in the army cadets and then the T.A. by joining the army in September 1977.

Enrolled into the Royal Artillery and having passed out of Woolwich as best recruit, he soon found himself attracting the attention of the regimental PTI in Hildeshiem, Germany, who encouraged his sporting ability by taking him under his wing and sending him on the courses required to qualify him as a PTI in his own right.

A tour of Northern Ireland in the summer of 1980 interrupted his progress, but by the start of 1981 Steven found himself at the school of PT based in Aldershot.

On the 11th July 1981, whilst taking part in the schools gymnastic display team, he over rotated, landed awkwardly and broke his neck, leaving him paralysed from the collarbones down.

During the 18-month hospitalization, he met and fell in love with a nurse and the world's media, brought about because 'The Church' initially refused them permission to marry due to Steve's disability, covered their marriage in 1984.

He quickly established himself within the local charity groups that offered help for disabled people and now chairs one of the biggest and fastest growing organisations in Derby, called 'The Disability Syndicate.'

As well as his role as chair of the group, he teaches medical students and psychology student's disability and equality issues, simply sharing his life.

He is still happily married and loves keeping himself as active as possible, despite the severity of his paralysis.

Lightning Source UK Ltd.
Milton Keynes UK
15 March 2011
169285UK00001B/16/P